Table Settings
For All Seasons

Table Settings
For All Seasons

In the Home and
In the Flower Show

BY JUNE PITTS WOOD

TABLE SETTINGS
ILLUSTRATING THE BOOK
BY
DEEN DAY SMITH
AND
JUNE PITTS WOOD

PHOTOGRAPHS BY RICHARD MOORE

Published by
THE NATIONAL COUNCIL OF STATE GARDEN CLUBS, INC.
4401 Magnolia Avenue, St. Louis, MO 63110-3492

Printed in the United States of America
by Columbus Productions, Inc.
Columbus, Georgia

First Printing 1995

ISBN 0-941994-10-4 (hardback)
ISBN 0-941994-11-2 (paperback)

Table of Contents

Dedication

- To my husband, Donald R. Wood, who has been my most constant supporter in every phase of my life.

- To our son, Alan, who played and slept under tables at flower shows from the age of three, while I worked there. As a man, he is still interested in all of my activities and is ever encouraging.

- To our daughter-in-law, Cindy, who helped me enter the world of computers. She has been so helpful and supportive.

- To Kathryn and Howard L. Pitts, the best parents anyone could have.

Foreword

My dear friends, June Wood and Deen Day Smith, have done it! While virtually every member of National Council of State Garden Clubs, Inc. has wished for a publication of this nature, I think it is altogether fitting that these two masters are the first to provide us with this solid reference material for successful table designs. It covers the full spectrum of table setting ideas, ranging from the pure and simple to the highly exotic and unusual.

June Wood is an accomplished Instructor in Design for Flower Show Schools and Symposia. Both she and Deen Day Smith are Master Flower Show Judges. Together they have more than a half-century of experience in award-winning flower arranging. Their combined talents have enabled them to produce this publication for the artistic and imaginative readers.

While each of us may pride ourselves on our ability to make things grow, it is what we do with the fruits of our efforts that truly distinguishes us. It is how we use the things we have grown to achieve harmony in our environment that identifies us as "experts". Now two of the world's most creative floral designers are sharing their knowledge, skills and abilities with their eager readers. We welcome this book for the sheer joy its beauty will bring to so many people.

Mrs. Graem Yates
President, *National Council of State Garden Clubs, Inc.*

Preface

For as long as I can remember, I have enjoyed setting a beautiful table, so I am drawn like a magnet to the china and housewares department of every department store I walk through. It is a very rare occurrence to attend a garage sale or visit an antiques shop without buying some dishes, glassware, or an interesting accessory to grace a table setting.

Table settings have become almost as compelling an interest for me as the flower arranging which first drew me to join a garden club. That is why the writing of this book has given me so much pleasure. In the past years a number of fine books on table settings have been published, but most of them are now out of print and are difficult to find. Many of them were not written with the flower show exhibitor or judge in mind. Hopefully, this book will fill that particular need, as well as the needs of the person seeking a source for creative "how-to-do-it" information on making inspired and attractive table settings for the home.

Without question, all of us live very fast-paced lives today. At a time when more and more women are working outside of their homes, it can be difficult to make that extra effort to set an attractive table after rushing home from a tiring day at work. It is a great temptation to eat a quickly prepared meal from trays while watching television. That is the usual routine in many of our homes today. As a result, families often must miss that time of sharing the day's experiences in a happy atmosphere around the dining table. It is hoped that this book will inspire its readers to add more pleasure and grace to their families' lives through good food, eaten from an imaginatively set table, even if it must, of necessity, be only on weekends and holidays.

The book is also aimed at those who gain great satisfaction from exhibiting and competing in flower shows, and in the judging of them. Most shows have classes or sections of table settings. The correct method for judging these exhibits is taught in the Flower Show Schools and Symposia sponsored by the *National Council of State Garden Clubs, Inc.* It is hoped that this book will be a source of needed information for students who attend those courses, as well as for the more experienced exhibitors and judges. Information presented in it is in agreement with that included in THE HANDBOOK FOR FLOWER SHOWS of the *National Council of State Garden Clubs, Inc.*

May each of you enjoy the creation of more beautiful and exciting table settings, with some help from this book.

June Pitts Wood
Albuquerque, New Mexico, 1994.

Acknowledgments

Deepest and sincerest thanks are due to Deen Day Smith for her work in coordinating the publishing of the book. Without her efforts the book would not have been published.

ALSO SPECIAL THANKS TO:

- Richard Moore: an artist with a camera, whose boundless patience and invaluable suggestions contributed immeasurably to the quality of this book.

- Hall's Wholesale Florist of Atlanta, Georgia, who supplied the beautiful plant materials for the table settings in the book.

- Ellen Griffin, who first appointed me to the Flower Show Schools Committee of *National Council of State Garden Clubs, Inc.*, where I have gained so much from shared knowledge and treasured friendships.

- Betty Belcher, a special friend, as well as a much valued advisor.

- Members of the Flower Show Schools Committee of *National Council of State Garden Clubs, Inc.* for 1993-95, and especially to Ann Milstead, Chairman of the Flower Show Schools Committee, and to Hallie Brown, International Symposia Chairman, for their careful reviewing of the text and photographs to assure compliance with THE HANDBOOK FOR FLOWER SHOWS.

- Willie Frank Webb and Jimmy Ogletree for their kind and patient assistance during the photographing of table settings for the book.

- Those friends in garden clubs throughout the United States and Mexico, friendships made in the course of almost thirty years of membership in garden clubs. They first planted the seed that I could, and should, write a book.

Thank you to *all* of you. You made it possible!

PART ONE:

How It All Began

CHAPTER 1.
A HISTORY OF TABLE SETTINGS

Setting the table is a task most of us perform every day, each day of the year. To many it is just a necessary chore, while to others it is an opportunity to exercise imagination and ingenuity. Since people have long associated good food with "the good life," eating that food from a lovely table setting enhances food's enjoyment, promotes a warm and relaxed atmosphere for conversation, and a close interaction among family members and friends. It also adds a much needed aspect of graciousness to our daily lives. Giving thought to setting the table well provides a creative outlet to each of us as we seek to add some needed variety, interest and "spice" to meals. That carefully set, creative table setting can turn any meal into one that is special, making every meal a celebration of sorts.

People have always "set" their tables to some degree, since it goes without saying that all people have to eat. We don't know how Eve presented food to Adam, but we can learn to some extent what table settings were like in times past by studying paintings and literature from those times. Haven't you ever wondered *why* we do certain things always in a certain way? *How* did we come to do these things?

It is only when man has reached a certain level of civilization that he can be concerned about such things as beautifying his surroundings and giving consideration to making his life more gracious. Table settings would certainly follow that pattern in their development and importance to daily life.

Egyptian Settings

On wall paintings in Egyptian tombs from 3,000 years ago, we can see food being presented to diners from tables adorned with lotus blossoms, which were laid on wooden trays or on baskets containing fruits and vegetables. This is evidence that flowers were used on dining tables, however there is nothing resembling an arrangement or "centerpiece" in these portrayals of dining scenes. Plates of wrought metals were used, as well as the trays and baskets. Paintings show goblets of wine and other drinks being offered. Of course, these paintings portray how life was lived among royalty and upper classes in ancient Egypt, but they show that grace and beauty were a part of those lives, even in such mundane acts as eating and drinking.

Some of the same tomb paintings do portray some very stylized arrangements, showing groupings of odd numbers of lotus blossoms, usually arranged in a rigidly upright manner in a shallow container, and with equal spaces between all flowers. The paintings do not show these arrangements in use on dining tables, however. Many historial researchers state these floral arrangements were probably intended for ceremonial use.

Greek Tables

Paintings in ancient Greek public buildings and temples portray scenes of dining, with garlands or wreaths of fruits and vegetables seen on the tables. Again, these plant materials are not organized into floral arrangements, but are used for their suggestion of abundance and plenty. Flowers were often strewn on the floor and even on tables for ceremonial occasions. These paintings have much to teach us about the presentation of food. Tables for dining in ancient Rome are patterned closely after those of the Greeks.

Settings in the 14th-18th Centuries

From the 14th century onward, we have many pictorial examples of how people lived, as well as dined. For example, there are large numbers of surviving paintings from the Medieval and Renaissance periods. From those times, we see pictures related to setting the table and of dining habits. It is interesting to contemplate that all of us in today's world enjoy comforts and luxuries which were unavailable even at royal courts in earlier times. We have all seen royal banquets depicted in paintings and movies. We see people sitting on stools and grabbing food from common serving dishes, then eating it with their hands. Allowing for a bit of artistic license, these are probably fairly accurate depictions of what 14th and 15th century dining was like.

Diners ate at heavy, primitive trestle-like tables, with stools or benches placed on only one side of the table. Many of us deplore what we perceive to be our uniquely violent society, but there is really nothing new in man's behavior from his earliest times to now. In Medieval and Renaissance times, this arrangement of stools or benches placed on one side of the table, with diners' backs near the wall, served a very practical purpose: when one's back was against a wall, an enemy or assassin could not approach from behind without being seen. The king or ranking person sat in the center with others on each side for the same reason — it was a more protected position. The prevalence of this type of table setting would tell us that assassination and violence were rather common occurrences, even if we had not read historical accounts of the period.

Those rough tables were usually covered with cloths, however, and many of those cloths were made from beautiful and elegant fabrics with elaborate draping. Large, heavy platters of food were placed on the table and everyone reached for whatever they liked, using their hands. The few available knives were placed on the table for the purpose of cutting off a portion of meat, and these knives were used by all. Hands were used for eating rather than forks because forks were very rare. At royal meals, guests usually did have individual plates. For less exalted households, plates probably would not have been present. Napkins also played a prominent role. These were large, and might be spread across the lap, but more commonly were tied around the neck.

Although in some paintings from these periods we do see vases containing bouquets of flowers, flowers are not seen in use on dining tables. There is no pictorial evidence that flowers were ever included as a part of the table settings during these times.

Gradually dining became more gracious and refined in the 17th and 18th centuries. Chairs had replaced stools at dining tables. Knives and forks were in more common usage. Royalty, aristocrats and people of wealth had sets of dining utensils specially crafted, and these were carried by their owners in fitted cases to the table for each meal. These implements were watched carefully and given extra care since they were much coveted and were not easily replaced. Napkins would be found on all tables. It is interesting to note, however, that napkins did disappear from tables for a time after forks became widely used. People assumed that because they were no longer eating with their hands, napkins should not be necessary. A titled European visitor to America in 1780 wrote, "A peculiarity of this country is the absence of napkins, even in the homes of the wealthy. Napkins as a rule are never used and one has to wipe one's mouth on the tablecloth, which in consequence suffers in appearance". This lack of napkins was soon found to be greatly inconvenient, and they reappeared.

It is not until the 18th century that we find evidence of arranged flowers being used on dining tables — "centerpieces" as they are often called today. In descriptions of tables from this period, the phrase *surtout de table* may be encountered. Translated literally, this means "above all", and refers to the placement of an exquisite and profuse table centerpiece at the head table of important banquets and dinners. The arrangement was usually placed on a *plateau*, which is a raised tray with a pierced gallery edge. It might be accompanied by tall candelabra and various statuettes or other accessories.

Epergnes were also used to hold the centerpiece on less formal occasions. In this period, epergnes were ornate silver stands with multiple branches, which supported small silver bowls or baskets. These, in turn, held fruits or sweetmeats. I have been especially interested in these since one of the premier designers and makers of 18th century epergnes was an English silversmith, Thomas Pitts. Such arrangements, typical of their times, may be seen in the period rooms at Colonial Williamsburg or other period homes and museums open to the public.

Artificial materials were much in use in the 18th century. These were considered to be lovelier and in better taste than were real plant materials. Many think that the Victorians had some sort of monopoly on the use of artificial materials, and that they were the first to use them. Not so! Many used artificial materials in the 18th century, the period which we now regard as the epitome of exquisite taste. The fake flowers were made of such varied materials as paper, silk, porcelain, enamel and ormolu, even sugar confectionery. This was the period when the Meissen and Sévres factories were at the peak of their artistry. They made magnificent porcelain flowers, but artificial, none the less.

The Victorian Period

Dining in the 19th century reached a state of ostentation and elegance not seen before or since. Even middle-class homes had servants, making possible enormous meals of numerous courses. The well-equipped Victorian table contained china, glassware and silver articles which we only see in museums and antiques shops today. Some of these things have uses obscure to most of us. Many people collect these decorative objects which were in everyday use in the Victorian age. They are objects of beauty in themselves, and their use can certainly make our table settings more beautiful and interesting.

There were ornate Art-glass pickle castors, castor sets for condiments, sweet-meat dishes, honey and preserve dishes — the list goes on and on. In the silver chests of the day, you probably would have found oyster forks, pickle forks, lettuce forks, sardine forks, asparagus forks, ice cream forks, fish forks, nut spoons, berry spoons, — and the list continued through many more kinds of specialized implements.

Besides such mundane china items as plates, platters, salad plates, bread and butter plates, cups and saucers, there were bone dishes, finger bowls, and even special sets for serving certain foods, such as ice cream sets, berry sets, tea sets, game sets (which depicted various game animals and birds), or fish sets, picturing many different types of fish.

In the Victorian period, flower arrangements were commonly seen on dining tables for "every-day" family dining, as well as for special occasions. Prior to this, flowers had been seen on tables in the 18th century, but only for rare and formal occasions. In Victorian times, it was the *expected* thing to have flowers on the table. The Victorian era was one in which adventurous plant collectors and explorers were bringing much unusual and exotic plant material back to England and the United States from all over the world, and these plant materials were widely used in flower arrangements of the period. Floral table decorations were full, cluttered, often over-done and utilizing an excessive number of accessories, but they were certainly enjoyed by those who created them and those who observed them. Unusual foliages, exotic blooms and garden-grown ones, fruits, and even artificial plant materials were used, along with accessories of every imaginable kind. During the Gay 90's, table settings and floral arrangements confined to one color or one type of flower were also considered to be the height of fashion.

In the late 19th century, public dining in restaurants became popular for the first time. Prior to this, men (and more rarely, women) ate at inns and pubs when traveling, and only as a last resort. For trips of just one or two days' duration, people usually preferred to bring food from home. In the late Victorian period, though, restaurant dining came into its own, and was often much more elaborate in the quantity of food and in its service than was eating at home. In this opulent age, food service reached its pinnacle in the restaurants of the period.

Tea time also became popular during the Victorian era, and it spread from England to America. This occasion demanded its own table appointments and rituals of service. Observance of tea time is again being promoted in various modern-day magazines, particularly in those encouraging an interest in things Victorian.

The Edwardian Age

The late 19th century into the early 20th century — during the reign of King Edward VII of England and his queen, Alexandra — was still a time of lushness and often excess, but table settings were simpler than they had been in the robust Victorian period. Art Nouveau and Oriental influences brought a lighter, more airy look to flower arrangements and to the table as a whole. Flowers were arranged with the incorporation of more space, thus escaping that "fully-packed" look of the Victorian era. Pastel colors were popular, as were fragrant flowers, such as sweet peas. This lightness and simplification did not extend to food, however, which was still presented in a bewildering number of courses, types and amounts.

Influence of Gertrude Jekyll and Constance Spry

When the name Gertrude Jekyll is mentioned, most knowledgeable gardeners think of her as being the designer of beautiful perennial borders, one who paid great and careful attention to color harmonies. She certainly was that. However, Miss Jekyll also wrote a book called FLOWER DECORATION IN THE HOUSE (1907), which had a pronounced influence on homemakers of that time. The arrangements in the book were a sharp departure in style from the still Victorian-influenced arrangements of the day. It probably would also influence flower arrangers of *our* time if more of them read her book, since much of it is still applicable. Miss Jekyll was a 'woman-of-all-seasons'. She not only grew magnificent flowers in her gardens at Munstead Wood in Surrey, England, but she also arranged them beautifully.

Her simple compositions were of beautiful flowers having delicate fragrances, fruits which had striking form or pattern, along with lovely foliages. (Miss Jekyll is credited with being the pioneer who first drew our attention to the beauty of gray-leaved plants, both in our gardens and in flower arrangements.) Being creations of Miss Jekyll, her floral arrangements also incorporated a wonderful sense of color. Those designs of hers would be as suited to most home settings of today, as they were to homes of that period in which they were created.

Mrs. Beeton, an English authoress, had great influence on the "home-arts" in the 1920's. She wrote a book entitled, MRS. BEETON'S FAMILY COOKERY AND HOUSEHOLD MANAGEMENT, which was widely used in many households of the time. A strongly Victorian influence is seen in her book, typified by her suggestions for huge meals of many courses, served from overly elaborate table settings. Table settings and flower arrangements pictured or described in the book are very similar to those which were prevalent in the Victorian period.

Constance Spry, another noted English flower arranger, introduced new ideas to the art of flower arrangement during the 1930's and 40's. Mrs. Spry was the owner of a fashionable flower shop in the Mayfair section of London, and the writer of a number of books on flower "decoration", as she preferred to call arrangements. At Wakefield Place, her home outside London, Mrs. Spry also conducted classes in "domestic sciences". Here she taught young society women to do all the things they had never done before in those servant-filled days of the past: such things as planning meals, cooking, setting a table, and serving a meal without help. "Doing the flowers" was also one of the things these enthusiastic young ladies learned from Mrs. Spry.

Constance Spry advocated freedom from the rules which had so long governed what was appropriate for use in a flower arrangement and on a dining table. She insisted that people should see the possibilities in *all* plant materials. She taught that arrangers should learn to appreciate each material solely for its color, texture or form, without having preconceived ideas about what things *should* or should *not* be used. She, along with Gertrude Jekyll and Vita Sackville-West, also is credited with a revival of interest in those roses referred to as "old-fashioned" or "old-garden" roses. She grew many of them in her garden, and used them in her arrangements.

Her table designs might contain such things as cabbages, tomatoes, autumn-tinted foliages in a bowl, or artichokes and dried hydrangeas heaped on a marble slab. These were plant materials formerly considered appropriate only to the kitchen or kitchen garden – they had never been used together before, and certainly never on a dining table! Constance Spry will be long remembered as an innovator, one who taught all of us to see the beauty in everyday plant materials and household items, and educated us to their use.

These ideas coincided with the tremendous growth of the garden club movement in the United States and of flower arrangement societies in Great Britain, both of which showed phenomenal growth in the 1950's. New trends and ideas begun then are still evolving and progressing today.

The 20th Century

The 20th century has seen enormous social changes which have affected the lifestyles of all but the very wealthiest of people. At the turn of the century, The Industrial Revolution lured many people who had previously worked as servants into better paying factory jobs. As a result, meals became simpler, with fewer courses or choices in foods. Meal service became less elaborate since servants were no longer available to do all the cooking, clearing and washing of the many table appointments, or the washing and ironing of fine table linens. World War I and the Depression accelerated this trend, so that women had to do most of those chores themselves which had previously been done by servants. The time-clock, another innovation of the times, played its part. Prior to this, there had not been the strict observance of "office hours" or "business hours", which came into being during this period. The business man who had previously enjoyed long leisurely breakfasts now rushed off to work in order to arrive there at an appointed time. Those long lunches, eaten at home while the office was closed, disappeared. These changes in lifestyles also dictated simpler meals and ways of serving them.

The dining room, which had once been a large and elegant room where all family meals were eaten, has now shrunk in size or been completely eliminated from many homes of today. In these homes, the dining room has simply become a dining "area", an extension of the living room or the kitchen.

Meals are now served in many different areas of the home, such as in the kitchen, a breakfast room or nook, the family room or den, the patio, terrace or porch, and even on small trays or tables in front of the television or in other rooms. Labor-saving devices such as washing machines and dishwashers have somewhat compensated for those lost servants from the past. We have simplified meal service by substituting mats in easy care materials for tablecloths which required meticulous ironing. For everyday use, we are more likely to choose casual dinnerware in materials such as stoneware, earthenware, pottery, metals, plastics, and occasionally paper, rather than the fine china which requires careful hand-washing. The same reason often dictates the use of heavier glassware or plastics instead of the delicate crystal which needs special attention. Many people of today who own fine quality table appointments find that these are kept for use only at holidays or for special occasions when more time can be given to their care.

The rush and stress of our modern-day lives often prompt a nostalgia for a slower, more gracious manner of living which we somehow believe existed in the past. As a result, many of us search dusty antiques shops and yard sales, or dig out old handed-down china from relatives, looking for those remnants of the past, such as the delicate antique flowered china or fine crystal stemware. People sometimes feel that the respect for quality and craftsmanship seen in these objects from earlier times is not present in many of the things offered for sale today, with the exception of the most expensive articles. This prompts many to seek out antique dining appointments.

The astute and creative person knows that it is no longer essential that everything must "match" in order for their appointments to be acceptable for use in an elegant table setting. Indeed, the mixing of varied pieces can add true distinction and originality to a table if the components are all compatible in color, texture and degree of formality.

It is hoped that this book will inspire thought, individual creativity and the desire to make daily life more interesting by making our meals more pleasant experiences, due in part to the lovely table settings from which they are eaten.

Fig. 1. A gracious table setting is shown in a beautiful dining room with antique furnishings. The spirit of the room is formal and traditional, and the table setting is highly compatible with it. "Flora Danica" china is used on fine white linen mats with metallic gold-bound edges. Flatware is gold, also in the "Flora Danica" pattern. (This table setting is obviously one which was set in a home-setting, and in this case, we would expect flatware to be seen on the table. *In a flower show, however, flatware is never permitted, not even on table settings entered in a Standard Home Flower Show.*) Lovely gold rimmed, cut-glass crystal stemware complements other appointments beautifully. Pink roses, yellow jasmine, and pink, yellow, and bright rose carnations are arranged in a large antique silver container. Colors in the floral design repeat those found on the china. The decorative unit is somewhat tall, but no place settings are set directly in front of it on either side of the table. The place settings on opposing sides of the table are set at each end of the decorative unit, so the people sitting across the table from each other can still see and converse across the table. (Deen Day Smith).

Part Two:

Practical Considerations

CHAPTER 2.
CHOOSING TABLE APPOINTMENTS
AND OTHER COMPONENTS

Suiting a Table Setting To Its Background: The Room Setting

Table settings are planned and their components selected after careful consideration has been given to the type of meal and where it will be eaten. The character of a room's setting (in other words, its degree of formality) will determine the type of meals to be served there and the appointments to be used. For example, in a formal dining room with brocade draperies and delicate antique furniture, it would hardly be appropriate to serve a meal of barbecued meat with beans, on rough burlap mats and heavy pottery dishes. The type of meal, table appointments and the room setting should all be compatible in style and degree of formality. This does not limit table settings to such an extent that they must *always* be of the precise style or period as the room in which they are used. An eclectic blending of appointments can be very interesting and beautiful, but that feeling of fitness and of belonging together, of being of similar quality, must always be present. In general, we may say that we should not create table settings which are a great deal more formal than the spirit of the room in which they are to be used, and the reverse is also true.

When planning table setting appointments for any room-setting, there are several elements of the room's background and décor which must be considered:

• The style and degree of formality of the *furniture*: Is the furniture of a particular period or style — Early American, Federal, Empire, Georgian, Victorian, French Provincial, Oriental, Contemporary, etc.? Is it of light or dark wood? Does it create an atmosphere of formality or a more casual one?

• What is the *background*? Are the walls painted? If so, what color? Are they light in tint, or dark in shade? Are the walls patterned, covered with fabric or wallpaper?

• What are the *draperies* like? Are they a solid color or patterned? Do they match the walls or contrast with them? What color are they? Are they of a heavy, opaque fabric or a more open, light-admitting weave?

- How are the *floors* covered? A solid colored carpet, or a patterned rug? Or is the floor bare? If bare, what is the material — wood, marble, tile, etc.?

- What kind of *lighting* does the room have? Is it bright or subdued? Where is the light-source placed: overhead, wall-mounted, concealed? Subdued and well distributed lighting adds much to a gracious atmosphere for dining.

- What kind of *accessories* are in the room? Are there paintings, mirrors and other objects of more or less permanent nature? If so, of what period or style are they; of what materials and colors? They, too, must be considered when choosing table appointments.

All of these things — the furniture, décor (style and period), and degree of formality of the rooms where meals are served are *fixed* and do not change without a good deal of effort and expense, so they will dictate your selections of dinnerware, flatware, glassware, table linens, table accessories and other components. These should all be carefully correlated in style/spirit, color and texture to assure harmony and suitability in table settings. Of course, there are varying degrees of formality — from the very formal to the most casual — and all of us should choose appointments that meet the needs of our own particular lifestyle and home-setting. We may covet fine and delicate china or crystal, but if they are never used, this would indicate that inadequate thought went into analyzing one's manner of entertaining and needs.

Table settings of today are much simpler and are different from those of our mothers and grandmothers. Lifestyles have changed, so that formality in entertaining is rare. The majority of meals are eaten in many different areas of the home, rather than always in the dining room. Appointments are often chosen to complement each other, but not necessarily to match. They may be of varying styles, shapes, colors, textures, but these eclectic choices still should be governed by one basic guideline: everything chosen should be compatible with everything else, and have that essential sense of being at one with the other, of each complementing the other.

Fashions change in appointments for table settings just as they do in everything else, but who says you have to follow blindly along with the crowd? Keep in mind that this year's fashion probably won't be next year's, so unless you can afford to indulge in temporary whims, think carefully before choosing such expensive items as dinnerware, flatware and crystal which have a design that may be outdated soon. If you *must* have that wild, uninhibited china you saw yesterday, then why not just buy some salad/dessert plates to add variety to things you own already, rather than buying an entire set of it?

In setting your table, keep in mind that it should be attractive; should be clean and crisp, and should be meticulous in its execution. By all means, exercise your imagination and creativity in putting together unusual tables, indulge your own personal tastes and preferences, but never forget the essential quality of good taste and appropriateness.

The Coordination of Components

Every functional table setting in the home has certain types of components which must be present if a meal is to be served and eaten comfortably: dinnerware ("dishes"), flatware ("silverware"), some kind of drinking utensils, and napkins. These appointments may be of infinitely varying materials — from fine china and crystal to heavier earthenware, thicker pottery and glassware, plastics, metals or even paper — but if a meal is to be served, these components should be present. Tablecloths or mats may or may not be used. If the tabletop is attractive and not easily damaged, the appointments can be set directly on the bare tabletop if desired.

As we have said, all chosen components should be the same in spirit and degree of formality, with harmonious colors, textures and scale. This is not to say that all table settings used in a particular room must always adhere rigidly to the same style and period, but settings will be much more successful if the departure is not too glaringly great. For example, it is unlikely that you would feel appointments had been correctly chosen and coordinated if a black and white roughly textured linen cloth, patterned with bold geometric shapes; heavy, shiny black square plates; unornamented stainless steel flatware with ebony handles; sleek black goblets; bright yellow linen napkins; and a decorative unit of black painted line materials combined with yellow sunflowers, would be suited to a dining room furnished with delicately patterned grayish-blue wallpaper, matching damask draperies, crystal chandelier, Aubusson rug and antique Louis XV furniture. Those described table appointments are all suited to *each other*, and would make a very attractive table setting in the right room, but they certainly would not be suitable for this particular dining room.

Texture, more than any other quality, will determine the degree of formality of any component. There should be enough variety in textures to assure interest and to avoid monotony, but all chosen textures should be within the same range of fineness or roughness. This is not difficult to understand. Each of you know that you would never choose a rough straw purse to accompany a satin ball gown. Burlap draperies would not be chosen for a dining room with damask wall coverings and exquisite antique needlepoint rugs. These kinds of selections are made in every area of daily living, so this same knowledge is employed when making choices of dining appointments.

Formality of color is usually determined by tint, tone or shade, and by the degree of intensity. A brilliant orange (full-intensity, or strong intensity hue), for example, would be quite at home in a more casual setting, while a soft peach (lower intensity tint, or weak intensity hue) would be a more suitable choice from within this same color family for a more formal, more elegant setting.

Picture first a dining room which has a dark walnut chair rail around it, with roughly textured, cream colored plaster walls above the chair rail. Below the rail is a cream, rough textured grass-cloth paper. The paned windows are covered with dark walnut louvered shutters instead of draperies. The floors are of old, polished, wide wooden boards, covered in turn with an oval beige, brown and rust braided rug. The furniture consists of a walnut trestle table, comb-back Windsor chairs and an antique corner cupboard. There are still-life oil paintings of fruits and flowers in dark, rich colors. The table is covered with a rust colored tablecloth of heavy linen. A hand-woven, fringed runner with stripes of rust, lighter shades of burnt orange, beige and brown is placed down the center of the tablecloth. The table is set with copper service plates, heavy beige pottery dishes with a rust band, and fairly thick amber glassware. The flatware is of stainless steel with wooden handles. There are beige napkins of a coarse linen with copper napkin rings. The centerpiece consists of dahlias of varying shades of orange, with line materials of dark bronze leucothe foliage, and lighter brown kiwi vines, all arranged in an antique wooden bread bowl. I hope you would agree that all of these are components which would be very much in keeping with a dining room of rather casual ambience.

Picture, then, another dining room. It has walls covered with cream damask and matching draperies with ornately draped valances. There is a fine crystal chandelier over a magnificent antique mahogany dining table, with mahogany ribbon-back chairs. The floor is highly polished wood, with an antique Oriental rug. It has faded into beautifully muted colors, primarily of soft apricot and deep aqua. This table is covered with a pale peach cloth under a fine ecru linen cut-work and embroidered cloth. The napkins match the cloth. Delicate ivory china is bordered with gold, and has a motif of lovely apricot flowers around the rim. Etched crystal of palest amber color matches the china in quality. The centerpiece consists of cream colored freesias, creamy roses, and pale apricot colored lilies, with delicate ferns used as filler material. These plant materials are arranged in a china compote which matches the china dinnerware. This is a table setting with colors from the same color-family as the informal one described in the preceding paragraph. Because of the difference in textures, and because tints of those same colors were used instead of colors at full intensity, this table setting would become an immensely more elegant one.

It is very rare nowadays for our tables to be formally set and for the accompanying service to be formal, since this is a style of entertaining now used primarily at State dinners and other governmental functions, or in homes of rarefied atmosphere. However, many homes are decorated in a fairly formal and traditional manner, and the less casual choice of components is more suited to them. Most of us use a semi-formal style of service only on special occasions and perhaps for certain holidays. For our daily meals, most of our table settings are much more casual and informal in character.

All of these things — our personal preferences, the atmosphere which we wish to create in our homes and with our table settings, and the style of entertaining we enjoy — will determine our choices in table appointments.

Dinnerware

China

China or porcelain is the finest quality of all the varied types of dinnerware. It is characterized by fine texture, translucence and hardness because it is fired at such an intense heat. It is not easily chipped and is not subject to crazing, but may be broken as the result of careless handling.

The Chinese learned to make porcelain in the 6th century, but the finest of hard, white-bodied porcelain made there dates from the Ming Dynasty, 1368 to 1643. European traders began to bring these Chinese wares to Europe and to England in the 16th century. The English called it "chinaware" for the simple reason that the first porcelain pieces were from China. The term still survives today, and is broadly, but incorrectly, used to describe *all* kinds of dinnerware.

By the mid-19th century, quality of Chinese porcelain was declining, but porcelain (or china) was being widely produced in Europe and England. A young German, Johann Böttger, found a successful way to produce hard-paste porcelain in 1709. The Meissen factory, using his formula, came into being in 1710 and is still in existence today, although only the china made in the so-called classical period (1720-1820) is correctly referred to as "Meissen". China manufactured by that same company since 1820 to the present is called "Dresden" china. Today, as it was "yesterday", Dresden china is of exquisite quality and is much coveted.

The blue and white Canton china, or "Chinese Export China", dating back to the 14th century, is highly prized by today's collectors. It was so popular when it first made its appearance in Europe and America that importers had a hard time supplying the demand for it. It was at one time even used as ballast in ships whose primary function was the importing of tea, so that more of the popular ware would be available for sale. Blue and white china based on the Chinese designs were produced by the Meissen factory (the "Blue Onion" pattern), Minton, Wedgwood, Johnson Brothers and many other china manufacturers in England ("Blue Willow"), as well as by Royal Copenhagen of Denmark ("Immortelle", or sometimes called the "Blue Fluted" pattern). The blue and white patterns based on the early Chinese patterns are still much in vogue today.

Very good china was also made in Holland, but that country is best known for its underglaze pottery, Delftware. It is named for the village of Delft, where it is still made today. A similar type of ware is made in Italy, Spain and Portugal, and is called Majolica; the French ware of the same type is called Faïence.

In England, Josiah Wedgwood made a type of hard, thin ware called "cream-ware", or "Queen's Ware", which became almost as popular as fine china. In 1806, Josiah Spode developed a ware called "stone china" which was much harder and finer textured than any other English ware made up to that time. He produced it in various patterns which imitated earlier Chinese ones. Spode's formula used calcined bones in the paste. His procedure was later adopted by the factories of Worcester (now called Royal Worcester), Minton, Doulton (known today as Royal Doulton), and Wedgwood. These factories are all still in existence, producing the famous English bone china. Other well-known firms are Coalport and Royal Crown Derby.

France was also producing beautiful, fine quality china at a number of factories in Limoges, beginning in 1783. Haviland China of Limoges still manufactures fine china. The founder of this factory was an American, David Haviland, who moved to France to start the porcelain factory. The Sévres factory was begun in 1756, and owed its great success to the financial help and patronage of Madame de Pompadour, mistress of King Louis XV. Madame de Pompadour was the arbiter of taste for her time, so it is fortunate that her taste was so exceptionally good. The Sévres factory still produces magnificent porcelains.

Other well-known producers of china in Europe are Capo di Monte and Richard Ginori of Italy; Royal Copenhagen of Denmark; Vista Alegre of Portugal; Herend of Hungary; and Dresden, Rosenthal and Nymphenburg of Germany.

America is represented in the world of fine china by Lenox. Franciscan and Pickard made exquisite china for many years. The White House chooses Lenox china for its tables, as it has since the turn of the century. The Japanese factories of Nikko, Mikasa and Noritake also produce high quality china.

China is made of refined clays which have been fired at a very high temperature so that the clay particles fuse to form a nonporous surface. In the past, china patterns had a traditional feeling with metallic bands or edges, delicate floral, or intricate Oriental patterns. Today, china is being offered in new colors and designs which reflect our more casual lifestyles, and are often departures from the more traditional designs of the past. The table settings shown on pages 15, 16 and 17 utilize fine china.

EARTHENWARE

Earthenware is *less* casual than pottery and *more* casual than china. It is fired at a moderately low temperature, so it is opaque rather than translucent, and is softer than china. All earthenware is fired twice. The first firing firms and sets the greenware piece, and the second one sets the glaze. Because earthenware is porous, it accepts color easily, and for that reason, often has brighter and more intense colors than is usually seen on fine china. It breaks and chips more easily than hard-fired china, but less than pottery. If struck, china has a clear bell-like tone, while earthenware and pottery will produce a dull, heavy tone. China is more durable than either of the other two types, but perhaps a dinnerware having casual charm is a more important factor for the buyer than is the greater durability of the more formal china.

Fig. 2. A very fine and elegant china, "Stafford Flowers" by Spode, is combined with delicate crystal. The lace tablecloth, linen napkin, exquisite china vase by Herend, and fine-textured plant materials are all in keeping with the china's quality. The colors of the pink carnations and purple caspia repeat those on the container, and are in harmony with those on the china. (Deen Day Smith).

Fig. 3. (at left) This setting has a strongly feminine and traditional character. The richly designed, floral patterned china sets the tone of the table. It is complemented by a cut-work tablecloth and napkins which employ embroidered motifs, using the same colors as those on the china and in the decorative unit. Exquisite crystal completes the setting. (Deen Day Smith).

Fig. 4. (above) The china in this setting is still elegant, but less formal than those settings in Figures 2 and 3. This plate is Oriental in its design and coloring. The Oriental theme is further carried out by the figural Chinese boy container, holding aloft a rhythmic design of contorted filbert, ti leaves, and "Stargazer" lilies. Linen napkins of two different colors and a sleek black modern goblet are in keeping with an attractive, less formal setting. (Deen Day Smith).

Fig. 5. A bright and cheerful setting uses earthenware dishes with colored, heavier textured glassware. The brilliant blue and gold of the dishes are repeated in the floral design of yellow lilies, white daisies, yellow pompon chrysanthemums, ferns and eucalyptus. The blue spiral-stemmed container adds a distinctive note, as does the butterfly napkin ring. (Deen Day Smith).

POTTERY

Pottery is heavy, thicker, lower-fired dinnerware which is porous and relatively soft. It is the most easily chipped type of dinnerware, so it is much less durable than china or earthenware. It does have its use in table settings, however. It uniquely fills the need for casual dining settings beautifully and in its own special way. It combines well with heavier glassware or drinking utensils made of pottery, metal or even plastic. It should be used with linens and plant materials of coarser textures.

Don't assume that pottery is always synonymous with inexpensive, and for that reason, devalue its contribution of beauty for use on certain kinds of table settings. We should never think of it as being just casual and coarse. Pottery, depending on its design, can be especially attractive and can bring real distinction and a feeling of quality to the table settings with which it is used. It may, depending on the artistry of its design, the quality of its craftsmanship, and the status of its maker, be as expensive as fine china.

Look for attractive and unusual pottery tableware at craft shows and sales, since a great deal of it is hand-made by individual ceramic artists. It is also manufactured in the United States, as well as Portugal, Spain, Italy, France, Germany, Sweden, Denmark, Japan, China, Mexico and other countries. Many of the companies which make fine china also manufacture pottery dinnerware.

Dinnerware may be found in other materials as well. Some examples are wood; metals, such as copper, brass or pewter or other alloys; plastics or paper. Paper is really only appropriate for the most casual of meals, such as barbecues, some alfresco meals or picnics, but there are some very well-designed paper goods available in shops now. Even tables set with this most casual of materials can be attractive and appealing.

The setting in which the meal will be served and the type of meal will determine what is appropriate. In referring to the type of meal, we are talking about the occasion, the time of day and the menu: all of these things will decide the appropriate degree of formality, and thus, what table appointments would be most suitable. For example, you would not serve hot dogs and soft drinks from delicate flower-edged or gold-banded china and fine crystal. Neither would you serve an elegant meal of roast pheasant and truffles on heavy pottery ware. Your innate good taste tells you this.

Selection of Dinnerware

When selecting dinnerware, most people's thoughts are directed immediately to the various patterns available, but selection of a particular pattern should not be the first consideration in choosing dinnerware. The first step should always be careful thought and analysis of how you live. Is your lifestyle more casual or formal? How do you usually entertain? Do you prefer casual backyard barbecues, or elegant sit-down dinners for a few friends, with soft lighting and quiet classical music? What is your family's make-up: numbers, ages, etc.? An active family made up of young adults with several small children will probably not live and entertain in the same manner as a middle-aged couple with no children living at home. After

Fig. 6. The swirling pattern on the brown pottery plate is repeated in that of the handled pottery soup bowl and on the decorative incised band of the tall pottery mug. A tall goblet, which matches the mug, serves as a container for the arrangement of dried coralbush shrub branches, orange "Enchantment" lilies and pachysandra. The block-printed napkin in shades of gold, brown and orange and the burnt orange placemat, hand-woven from heavy yarn, are compatible in texture and in character with other appointments. The cheerful rooster and hen figurines repeat colors and textures found in the other components. (June Wood).

A group of different types of dinnerware is shown in Fig.7. There are two examples of fine china in the middle of the top row, as well as plates of earthenware on the right and some of different materials such as metal, plastic and paper on the left side. On the bottom row, the Easter egg plate and the two in the center of the row are pottery dishes. Others in the bottom row, of both earthenware and china, illustrate those pieces having interesting shapes and patterns which might be mixed with other dinnerware to introduce variety and interest to a setting.

giving consideration to these questions, you will then be able to decide what type of dinnerware will best meet your present needs: fine china, earthenware, or pottery. Only after making these decisions, based on careful analysis, are you ready for the pleasure of choosing a specific pattern.

The trend today is away from complete, matching sets of dinnerware and toward choosing varied pieces with different shapes, colors and patterns to mix with the dinner plates. All should be compatible in texture and colors, whether these are matching or contrasted. Most dinnerware today is referred to as "open stock", which means individual pieces can be purchased separately rather than as complete sets. This makes it easier to replace needed pieces, as well as to mix, match or contrast dinnerware pieces to create unique place settings.

"Starter" sets, consisting of four place settings — usually twenty pieces — are often seen in stores. "Completer" sets of such extra pieces as bowls, platters, salt and peppers, creamers and sugars are also sold. China may also be bought by place settings or as individual pieces.

Another option might be that of choosing china by *courses* rather than as an entire matched set. For example, there might be round, rimless salad plates with a design of mixed flowers in an all-over pattern; the main course might be served on a creamy china with a motif of delicate flowers of the same colors as those on the salad plates, but only around the rim; dessert might be served on square, solid-colored plates in one of the colors featured on the other pieces from previous courses, and coffee might be served from cups and saucers which match the pattern used for the main course. Bread and butter plates should match the dinner plates. Possibilities and combinations are endless when following this plan for selection of appointments. There are only a few restrictions which should be kept in mind. There should be no mixing of fine china, earthenware, or pottery. If choosing appointments by courses, they should all be of the same degree of "fineness". Only shapes, patterns and/or colors would be mixed, never *types* of dinnerware. You might, however, choose colored glass plates for one or more of the courses in a pleasingly coordinated color and of a similar quality as the dinnerware if you wished.

Having made these important decisions about what type, quantity, and make-up of dinnerware you need, you will then be ready to go shopping for the specific dinnerware you want. Keep in mind that it is not the price of the materials which will determine the cost of dinnerware, as is often the case in the various types of flatware. Instead, the cost will be determined by the manufacturing process, the fine technique and artistry of the decoration, and by the prestige of the company whose name accompanies it. In deciding on a style, shape, color, pattern, etc., keep in mind that you will be using this dinnerware for quite some time, and you want to be happy with your choice over time. Choose an attractive, appealing shape and pattern. Unless you are in the happy circumstance of having enough money (and storage space, which is not an incidental consideration!), avoid one which is of such flamboyant color and/or pattern that you will soon become tired of it if it is to be used every day, or at least, often. Select one from an established company, so that you will be able to buy more pieces in the future when you want to expand the number of your place settings or to replace broken pieces. Above all, select one which is in keeping with the style and character of the room, or rooms, where you will be using the dinnerware.

Care of Dinnerware

Special attention should be given to the care and storage of dinnerware. If possible, fine china should be stacked with felt pads between each piece. If not, at the very least a folded paper napkin should be placed between them. Never slide one plate across another. Place them one at a time on top of each other without sliding in order to avoid scratches. Cups should be hung from cup hooks or set individually on the shelf. They are too easily broken if stacked.

All dinnerware should be washed in hot soapy water, avoiding cleaners with harsh abrasives. Some foods which contain high levels of acids, such as lemon juice, oranges, pineapple or vinegar may damage some colors, so china should be washed as quickly as possible after those foods have been served. If dinnerware has become stained, it can be cleaned by rubbing gently with a soft cloth to which a small amount of toothpaste, containing brighteners meant for cleaning dentures, has been added. Wash immediately after using this. To give the best possible care to your dinnerware, it is necessary to know whether the decoration on the ware is underglaze or overglaze. If it is underglaze, the pattern is protected by a glaze fired over it, but if it is overglaze, the pattern is applied on top of the glaze. Overglaze pieces are usually much more easily damaged.

For safety's sake, it is very important to buy dinnerware which is lead-free. Some imported pieces, particularly those of earthenware or pottery, have been found to have high lead contents in their glazes. Red glazed ones can be particularly toxic. The government is attempting to screen these wares, but you should look for a label which states that the ware is lead-free.

Drinking Utensils

Like the generic term, "china", many people refer to all glassware as crystal. However, to be correct and precise the term, "crystal", should only refer to the very finest and thinnest quality of glassware. Fine crystal has a high percentage of lead in its make-up, which gives it that clear, sparkling luster and light-reflective quality. Lead in crystal, unlike lead in dinnerware, is safe since it does not leach out into the liquids it holds. Glassware plays an important role in our table settings other than the utilitarian one of holding liquids for drinking. It adds brilliance, sparkle, glamour and beauty to our settings in a way which no other components can do. It also introduces a variation in height when compared to the flatness of the dinnerware. It provides a feeling of lightness to the setting to off-set the heaviness of dinnerware and flatware.

Glassware may be *blown* or *pressed*. Blown glass is usually more delicate, more brilliant, and more highly polished than pressed glass, which usually is heavier and less expensive than blown glass. Fine glassware may also be cut, which is pains-takingly done by skilled artesans.

The Italians were the first to create fine glassware having exceptional decorative style on the island of Murano, near Venice. They perfected techniques which allowed them to produce thin, delicate glass pieces. Later, fine glass was produced in Germany, Bohemia, England and Holland. Today, wonderful glassware is produced in America, Italy (still in Venice), in France at the Baccarat and Lalique factories, in Ireland by Waterford, and in Sweden by Orrefors. Many of the American, European and Japanese companies which manufacture fine china also produce high quality crystal. Interesting, but less expensive glassware is manufactured in Mexico, Spain, Portugal, Japan and China, as well as in other countries.

In the United States, a number of glass factories in West Virginia, such as Blenko, Fostoria, Viking, and Pilgrim produce quality glassware. Crystal from West Virginia was chosen for use in the White House during President Kennedy's administration. Prior to that, glassware used in the White House came from Europe, but Jacqueline Kennedy wanted to emphasize the use of American-made products.

Lenox China makes high quality glassware. A number of other glassware companies in the United States make less expensive, but good quality glassware. Libbey Glass is one example. Exquisite antique glassware also may reward the diligent searcher – such fine examples as glassware made by Steuben, Corning, Heisey, and Sandwich Glass Companies, among many manufacturers of excellent quality glass.

The degree of formality of any glassware is determined by its thickness/thinness, its design , and its type or style. The type refers to the purpose or use: whether it is a stemmed goblet, a tumbler, a juice glass, parfait, water, wine, etc. The design of glassware has several points to be considered : its shape, proportion, any superimposed decoration such as bands, etching, cutting, etc. In general, thin glassware which is stemmed or footed is more formal than tumblers, and also is more formal than those same styles if made of heavier, thicker glass. More formal ware often has metallic banding, etching or cut patterns. Less formal glass, if patterned at all, usually has its pattern pressed into it. Textured glassware is informal, while more formal ware is always smooth in texture.

Clear, elegant glassware has a unique and lovely quality of its own, but colored glassware has a very special charm and appeal, too. It may emphasize one of the colors seen in the dinnerware, or it may introduce a note of color-contrast or accent. Until fairly recently, colored glassware was only considered suitable for less formal tables. Most fine crystal in the past was expected to be clear. Today many exquisite crystals are colored, and they are indeed beautiful. Colored glassware adds an extra note of festivity and gaiety to a table setting.

Selection of Glassware

If you are just beginning to acquire a selection of glassware for use in your home, three types of glasses are probably adequate for most needs: a tumbler (or a low-footed glass or a stemmed goblet) for water and other beverages, juice glasses, and sherbet glasses for desserts. Stemmed goblets, even when made of heavier and thicker glass, are more fragile and more easily broken than tumblers, but stemware of this style does add a degree of elegance even to an informal or casually-set table. For durability's sake, you might also prefer glass bowls instead of stemmed sherbet glasses for desserts.

Fig. 8. A variety of different kinds of drinking utensils are shown. In the middle of the back row are fine crystal pieces: clear, cut and gold-banded, as well as a dark violet one with a clear stem. To the right of those is a group of less formal ones which are of good-quality glass and are relatively thin, but are not fine crystal. To the left of the crystal in the back row is a group of attractive plastic pieces. (Plastic is not easily broken, but is very easily scratched.) Plasticware is for use in more casual settings. On the left side of the bottom row is a grouping of casual, heavier glassware. In the middle are pottery mugs, and on the right, some utensils of other materials, such as brass, silver and wood. Drinking utensils are chosen for suitability to setting, occasion and compatibility with the other components to be used on a particular table.

Later you might add iced tea glasses or wine glasses. Choose glassware that is of the same style and degree of formality as your dinnerware and other appointments. If selecting a colored glassware, be sure that it is of a pleasingly blending or contrasting color to your dinnerware. It is usually better to choose glassware that is not too ornate or too heavily patterned. These simpler designed pieces can be used with a much wider variety of other appointments. Buying things which are interchangeable with a good many of the other things you own is sound economy, and will also give you more versatility and pleasure in the long run.

Drinking utensils are not necessarily confined to glass. They may be of pottery, china, wood, metals, plastic or paper, if compatible to the other components on your table in degree of formality, suitability to occasion, color and texture.

Flatware

For ease and precision in communication, the tools with which we eat are referred to as flatware. However, many people use the broader term, "silverware", to refer to these things, no matter what materials the tools are made of, because originally such tableware was made of silver. Today they might be made of stainless steel, bronze, gold-plate or some other alloy, or even plastic. In England, cutlery is the term used for these utensils.

Early man used shells for eating. As his skills progressed, he added wooden or bone handles to these shell implements, and the first spoon was created. Later the entire piece was made of carved wood. The first metal spoons were created about four thousand years ago by the Egyptians, who had learned to refine and work with silver as well as other metals. It is told in Chapter 25 of the Book of Exodus that God instructed Moses to make golden spoons for the tabernacle. The Greeks and Romans made spoons of bronze and gold. Probably the most elegant such things to ever be made were crafted by the Italian Renaissance artist, Benvenuto Cellini of Florence.

The first knife was made of stone and was used as a hunting weapon. Later, knives were made of bronze and iron. It was not until the Middle Ages that evidence is found of knives being used for eating as well as for hunting. Fork-shaped objects were also used as weapons in earlier times. The first ones made for eating utensils were probably just forked sticks, then later they were carved from wood. These same fork-like tools probably were also used to hold food over a fire for cooking.

In Renaissance times, people carried their eating utensils with them. These were never provided on the table — each person was expected to provide his own for meals. Spoons and forks were carried in cases, while the knife was carried in a scabbard attached to the belt. More affluent people had silver utensils, while the less affluent had pewter ones. Copper and brass were also used as silver substitutes. Knives and forks first appeared in general use on tables in Italy in the 1500's. They became widely used in England and France in the 1600's. The English did not accept this new custom readily. Eating with utensils was considered effeminate, and the clergy preached against their use as being a heretical substitute for "God-given fingers". The first fork was imported to America by Governor Winthrop in 1633. It is said that President George Washington's mother, Mary Ball Washington, considered the use of forks vulgar, and would allow only knives and spoons to be placed on her table.

Even today, some cultures may use flatware to a lesser extent than others. Long-term custom might favor food being eaten with the hands, with other types of eating tools, or breads may be the main conveyor of foods. For example, in Mexico, in other Latin American countries, and in some parts of the United States, some types of food may be scooped with tortillas; in India and many African countries, bread is used to convey food to the mouth; and in most Asian countries, chopsticks are used rather than knives and forks. In Thailand, forks and spoons are used, with knives playing a much less important role, since most foods are chopped into bite-sized pieces when they are prepared.

Early knives were rounded on the tip to prevent their use in assassinations. It was discussed in Chapter 1 how the arrangement of tables and the placement of dignitaries and rulers at the table were dictated by the need for security. During this time the blade was made of steel, with only the handle being made of silver. This practice is continued today because silver, being a much softer metal, is more easily damaged as well as being less strong. Knife handles also became works of art, being made of such materials as ivory, amber, horn, enamel, rock crystal and various other precious and semi-precious stones. They were major status-symbols of their time. Traveling sets of eating utensils were still carried in their special cases as late as the end of the 17th century.

Selection of Flatware

Flatware is often the most expensive part of the table setting, so it should be chosen very carefully. Such an investment will be in use for a long time, so you want to be sure that your choice is one you will be happy with over a long period of time, particularly if this choice is to be your only or primary set of flatware. Consider your lifestyle, how you prefer to entertain, and the room setting where most of your meals will be served. The pattern of the flatware should coordinate well with the chosen china and crystal, as well as other components, such as linens, accessories, etc.

Instead of silver, which is the most expensive choice, many people of today are choosing stainless steel. At one time, stainless steel was considered to be the poor man's substitute for sterling silver. Today it is being made in a wide selection of patterns and finishes and has a degree of elegance within itself, but it is still generally used for more casual dining.

Flatware is also made of bronze in Thailand and other Asian countries. This, too, can be very attractive, but is only compatible with certain dinnerwares since it is usually strongly Oriental in its design. Gold-plated flatware is attractive with certain china and crystal which have gold bands or other trim. Some lovely flatware has mother-of-pearl handles or colored handles made of various materials. You may find some especially beautiful mother-of-pearl or porcelain handled flatware in antiques shops if you look for it.

Select your flatware for its own beauty and appeal, as well as for its compatibility to your other appointments. It, too, can be assembled by place settings, by entire sets, or as individual pieces. A basic place setting consists of five or six pieces: dinner knife, dinner fork, salad/dessert fork, soup spoon, teaspoon and butter spreader. Such pieces as dessert spoons, iced tea spoons, luncheon knives and forks, cocktail forks, and other miscellaneous pieces which are nice to own, but not essential, can be added later if you wish.

Patterns which are less ornate are easier to clean and to take care of, so this should be considered if your time is limited. These simpler types of designs also lend themselves more readily to combination with other appointments. Pleasing proportions and comfort in shape, size and weight are also points to be considered in making your selection.

Serving pieces made of silver are called *hollowware*. These are such items as coffeepots and teapots, candelabra and candle sticks, pitchers, gravy boats, bowls, salt and pepper shakers, goblets, vases, etc. These pieces get their shapes from spinning of the silver, while flatware is cast in molds. Hollowware may also be silverplate over some alloy, such as brass or copper.

Care of Flatware

Sterling silver flatware should not be stored and kept only for special occasions. It is very durable, so should be used often, if not everyday. It will acquire a beautiful patina if used often. It should not be washed in the dishwasher, however, where it may be pitted, permanently stained, spotted, or severely scratched. If your time-demands limit you to things which can only be washed this way, then it would be safer to use your precious silverware only for those times such as holidays and special occasions when you can give it the care it deserves.

Fine silverware deserves special care. It should be washed soon after use in hot soapy water, and dried thoroughly. It should never be allowed to just drain or air-dry since it may dry with spots. If salt, acids or fatty foods are left on it for some time, pits may appear on the silver which cannot be removed. Salad dressing, eggs and rubber of all kinds will cause deep tarnish or a permanent stain if left in contact with silver, so rubber bands, for example, should never be carelessly tossed into a silver piece. Silverware should be stored in as airtight an atmosphere as possible to prevent tarnish. Store it in a dark place, wrapped in flannel or specially treated tarnish-resistant cloth. Silverplate is treated in the same way as silver. Stainless steel does not tarnish, and does not need to be treated as carefully. Bronze will also tarnish over time.

Silverware is never used on table settings in a flower show because of the concern for security. The schedule might permit inexpensive, disposable utensils, such as those made of plastic or chopsticks to be used. Most of the tables shown in this book do not show silverware on the tables. The two exceptions are the settings seen in Fig. 1. and Fig. 58, which are tables in home settings and are not designed for entry in flower shows. The Oriental setting in Fig. 49 shows a celadon soup spoon. This is certainly not in the same category as expensive flatware, but the show's schedule would determine whether it could be used.

Table Linens

The term "table linens" refers to any fabric used for table covering: any cloth, place mats, runners and napkins used on a table. They may, of course, be made of linen, but they might also be of lace, cotton, synthetics, metallics, or a wide variety of other types of fabrics. These, too, are chosen for their suitability to the room setting and for compatibility to other components in degree of formality, color and texture.

The Bible mentions linen as a table covering, and fine linens have always had a special air of luxury and quality about them. Even in earlier times, luxurious linens were used on the tables of those who could afford them. In the Middle Ages, tablecloths were referred to as "borde cloths" because dining tables at that time were simply boards placed on trestles, hence the term "borde cloth", for the covering used on such a table. The word "tablecloth" is not encountered in common usage until in 16th century England.

Sometimes the tables shown in early paintings have much draping of the table coverings. In many early paintings, particularly English ones, tables are shown covered with "Turkey" carpets; presumably these had been imported from Turkey. This may account for today's trend in which we see tables covered with fine handmade quilts in decorator magazines. It is hoped that no one would actually eat on such a covering, since a beautiful and irreplaceable object could be seriously or permanently damaged.

Our ancestors felt that a table was only properly "dressed" if it was covered with a fine linen, damask, appliquéd organdy, embroidered linen, lace or cut-work cloth. For more informal meals, the table would have been covered with a cotton or linen cloth of heavier weight or coarser texture, probably embroidered or otherwise embellished by some talented needlewoman in the family. Most people today use these fine linens (or informal vintage ones) only for special entertaining or especially important occasions. Many of us feel that we do not have the time to give such linens the special care they require, so for day-to-day meals, most people use easy-care cloths or place mats, or else appointments are set on the bare tabletop.

Except for such fine linens as antique Venetian or French lace, exquisite cut-work or hand-embroidered cloths, linens are not nearly as expensive (and thus permanent) investments as are china, flatware and fine crystal, so this is one area in which the greatest variation can be made in your table settings. A change in the color of your table coverings is one of the easiest changes you might make in your table components. Linens which you are tired of can be given new life and personality by dying or tinting them a different color. Anyone with the ability to sew can make tablecloths, mats and runners quite easily and inexpensively. Those of contrasting prints in related colors can be especially appealing. Fabric shops are full of beautiful textiles, and it is often easier to make a more distinctive and totally "right" table covering than it is to find and purchase the cloth you need for particular table appointments. Table coverings may also be layered for special effects, such as lace or cut-work ones used over colored undercloths to emphasize their patterns. Dark colored table linens add drama to a table setting because they provide maximum contrast in color, but care must be taken that they do not overpower the entire table setting.

It is also true that table coverings may be of many different materials other than fabric. They might be made of straw, vinyl, plastic, cork, bamboo, even mats cut from plate glass in pleasing shapes. There are many different types of interesting and beautiful table coverings which may be made or purchased relatively inexpensively, and they can give your table setting a whole new look.

Any table coverings may be finely textured or coarse; dull or shiny; solid in color or patterned. In general, a plain cloth or mat will usually be more pleasing with dishes that are patterned, and vice versa, even though it is the current fashion to combine appointments of various patterns. When using multiple patterns, you must be very careful to avoid a busy, uncoordinated look to your table setting, which destroys its sense of harmony and unity.

Whatever kind of table covering is chosen, these components are not usually "stars" within themselves. Cloths, runners or mats are the background for other components, and are meant to show those appointments to the greatest advantage without calling undue attention to themselves. There are exceptions to every "rule", of course. If your tablecloth is one of exquisite material and craftsmanship, it may well be the featured component, with other appointments playing supporting roles. In the final analysis, the only determining factors will be compatibility with other components and the room's setting.

It is possible that no tablecloth or mat will be used if the table's top is attractive and not easily damaged by heat, stains or moisture. Setting the components directly on a highly polished wood, marble or glass table can be very lovely and elegant. If a tablecloth is used, think of it as being the background against which all table appointments will be seen, since diners in actual settings and viewers in flower show settings will be looking down at the cloth and other appointments. For that reason, it is very important that the tablecloth be compatible in color, texture and pattern with all other components.

The decorative unit, unless it is a very low, horizontal design, will be taller than other appointments such as dishes, glassware, etc., and will have no *immediate* background directly behind it. It will be seen against what would be considered to be a *distant* background: furniture, walls, windows, draperies, etc. of the room in which the table setting is placed. In a home setting, this distant background should certainly be considered, and the designer does have a good deal of control over it. In a flower show setting, the distant setting would be any other table settings, flower arrangements, show staging, walls of the show room, any other types of exhibits, as well as people in the show room, which the eye will take in simultaneously while looking at any single exhibit. The exhibitor has absolutely no control over the distant background or any prior knowledge of what most of it will be like, so the distant background is disregarded when planning for her or his own table setting exhibit, as well as when any exhibit is judged.

Even more than color, *texture* determines the degree of formality of table linens, as well as that of other appointments. Fine china and crystal demand a fine-textured fabric, such as damask, fine lace, organdy, etc., while more casual earthenware and pottery need a coarser textured fabric in order for components to be in keeping with each other.

The shape of the dining table (square, oval, round, etc.) will dictate the shape of the tablecloth, and you should allow an overhang of from twelve to eighteen inches on all sides to avoid a too-skimpy appearance. An underlay which is longer than the tablecloth may be used, with the table covering and the underlay being of different colors, thus complementing each other and introducing a more creative use of color.

Floor-length cloths really should only be used on buffet tables, tea tables or reception tables since it is not possible to eat comfortably or safely if the table overhang is bunched up in diners' laps. It is also very possible that someone may trip on the floor-length cloth, causing the tablecloth and other appointments to be pulled from the table, resulting in an expensive as well as highly embarrassing accident.

If mats are used, usually an adequate spacing between settings would be twenty-four inches (24") from the center of one mat to the center of adjacent ones. A place mat should be large enough to hold the entire place setting without crowding. It is not an absolute requirement that all appointments be on the mat, however. If size does not permit everything to be on the mat without excessive crowding, then any items not on the mat should be placed as near to it as possible so there is no question about which items belong to a particular place setting.

Mats may be of any shape — round, square, oval, hexagonal, triangular, fan-shaped, or any other interesting shape. They may never overlap each other on the table. For an orderly and attractive appearance, each one's edge should be placed approximately one-half inch from the edge of the table, unless a round one of a soft fabric is more attractive hanging slightly over the table-edge. It is very important that all place mats on the table be placed at the same distance from the table's edge for the sake of uniformity.

Place mats are acceptable for use for all occasions except the most formal ones, or for buffet tables, tea tables and reception tables. They are made in a wide variety of materials, from the most casual ones of coarsely-woven yarns, straw, cork, plastic or wood to the most elegant lace, embroidered linen, organdy, silk or cut-work. What is used will be dictated by the room setting, the occasion, and by the other chosen components.

Napkins are the one item of table linens which are essential on all tables in the home. Napkins were used from very early times — in fact, they were more essential then than they are today, since most meals were eaten with the fingers. With the advent of wide-spread use of forks, napkins disappeared for a time from English tables as well as those of Colonial America, since one no longer ate with the fingers. It was soon realized that they were needed, however, even if one was so fortunate as to own forks and other eating implements.

No *actual* meal can be eaten comfortably without a napkin. In flower shows, however, for either Functional or Exhibition tables, the HANDBOOK FOR FLOWER SHOWS has now been amended to read, "napkins *may* be used on all tables". Most exhibitors will probably want to include napkins on Functional settings in flower shows, since napkins are needed for actual functional settings, but in the final analysis, whether napkins are included on tables in flower shows or not is the exhibitor's choice.

Most napkins sold for use on luncheon tables are about fifteen inches (15") square. For more formal tables, the napkins should be larger. Napkins for tea tables are smaller and more dainty. Napkins on informal tables may match, blend or contrast with the other linens. For semi-formal settings, napkins may match or blend in fabric and in color. For formal tables, the napkins should match. Cloth napkins are used for formal, semi-formal, and most informal occasions, but paper may be used for the most informal ones.

In flower shows, more than one napkin may be used together for special color effects. These may be used on either Functional or Exhibition Tables. Of course, this may also be done for table settings in the home if desired. Napkins may be folded in any manner that is neat and attractive, that fits the occasion, and that enhances the overall setting. Usually they are folded in the traditional oblong fold on semi-formal and formal tables.

Napkins may be placed on the table in any manner you choose to complement the overall setting, depending on the formality of the occasion. For formal or semi-formal settings, the napkin is either placed in the center of a service plate or to the left of the plate. For more informal settings, the napkin may be placed anywhere you desire for attractiveness and convenience. It is always true that napkins used in Exhibition Table Settings may be placed wherever the exhibitor chooses, to balance the overall design or to add interest to the design.

Care of Table Linens

Fine linens which are stored for considerable lengths of time between uses should not be starched, as this can damage the fabric's fibers and can also cause yellowing. If they are stored folded in a drawer, they should be taken out and refolded periodically in order to avoid damaged fibers and the creation of more permanent creases. The best way to store linens is by rolling on a large dowel, carpet roll, or mailing tube. In this way, creases can be avoided. All stains should be removed promptly, or else they may become permanent. Any linens used on dining tables must be immaculately clean and well-pressed. One length-wise seam in the center of a table cloth is permissible, but there should be no other creases, and certainly no wrinkles.

Selection of Table Linens

When you stop to consider it, table linens assume a special importance in table settings because they cover such a large area. They demand a lot of attention for themselves, due to sheer "weight" of proportion, as well as being the background against which other appointments are seen. For that reason, the cloth should be well-related to the other components in texture, pattern, and in color.

As in the selection of other appointments, unless you have a good deal of money to invest in them, tablecoverings should be of a color and texture which you will find enjoyable over a period of time, and which you will not tire of quickly. Very highly-patterned ones in exotic and strong colors, very dark colors, or shiny textures such as metallic cloths may be exciting for an occasional appearance, but you probably would not like to see them on a daily basis. It is true, however, that table linens are not nearly as long-term an investment as china or flatware, so you can indulge flights of fancy with them with fewer twinges of conscience than you can with the other appointments.

In selecting table coverings, consider these points:

- If *patterned*, avoid too much busyness. A highly-patterned cloth will often clash and be in too much competition with most other components.

- If *colored*, choose those which blend, match or contrast pleasingly with those appointments with which they will be used.

- Consider their *appropriateness* to the room setting where they will be used, as well as to occasions where they will be used (casual, informal, or semi-formal).

- What about *durability*? How will the coverings stand up to repeated launderings? Are they really practical? If it is a cloth which must be cleaned, rather than one which can be washed, that is another consideration which must be made when you think about its true cost, and this is not just the price which the store is asking for it!

- Think a bit more about *practicality* – practicality and durability are not necessarily one and the same. Picture a rough-textured straw mat or a pebbly-textured plastic mat. These materials are long lasting, therefore durable, but if they are to be used on tables at which small children – notoriously messy eaters – will be served, then they are not practical. You may, at this point, be disagreeing, but I can assure you that this is true. Mats with those described surfaces cannot be just wiped with a damp cloth if food is spilled on them. The food will get down into the various cracks and crevices and become almost impossible to remove.

You may be thinking, "But these are such inexpensive types of table coverings, why not buy them!". Are they really? If you pay just five dollars each for them, and they are ruined after only a few meals, then simply throwing twenty or thirty dollars in the trash makes just as much economic sense as buying place mats which will have to be thrown away after a very short time. Why not look for those which have a more practical, easier to clean surface while children are small, and buy those other less practical ones when your children are a bit older and have become more skilled eaters? There are just as many lovely things available to buy which are practical for your present needs as there are impractical ones. It simply takes a little more careful thought and looking in order to find them.

Table coverings should, of course, be of the correct size and shape for the table on which they will be used. Take your table's measurements with you when you go shopping so you won't have to guess about correct sizes, and remember to allow enough for a graceful twelve to eighteen inch overhang. Since making lovely table settings are a particular interest of mine, I never leave on a trip without making sure that I have the measurements of all my tables in my purse, as well as a tape measure, so I can double-check those appealing hand-made things that I may find in street market stalls. After all, I can't easily run back to Germany or Hong Kong to exchange them if they don't fit, and neither can you. Even that interesting cloth found on sale at a local department store is not always readily returnable.

Having a varied selection of table coverings is a relatively inexpensive, easy way to add variety and diversity to your other table setting appointments, and they will make your entire setting seem to be a new one.

Accessories

According to the HANDBOOK FOR FLOWER SHOWS, an accessory is "an object or objects added to the decorative unit(s) or overall table design. Accessories may be used for all types of tables". On a dining table such things as figurines, candles, cigarette holders or ashtrays, salt dishes, salt and pepper shakers, candy or nut dishes, decanters, etc. would be considered accessories. There are no rules of etiquette which govern their use, other than the requirements of good taste – that they be suitable for the occasion and to the setting.

Accessories can add beauty, originality and distinction to an otherwise rather ordinary setting. You should exercise some self-control, however, since using too many will create a distractive and cluttered appearance to your table. As in the choice of all other appointments/components, accessories must be in keeping with the table's room setting and suitable for use with all other components on the table in spirit, degree of formality, color, scale and texture.

Accessories should only be used when they truly play a needed part in the overall design of the setting and are well-integrated into it. They may help in establishing a particular theme for a party or for a holiday table. They should not be added simply because their owner thinks them beautiful or cute, or because they have some sentimental association. They should be placed in such a way that they aid, rather than disturb, the overall balance of the table, and so they do not interfere with comfortable conversation or dining.

In many of the tables pictured in this book, you will see examples of accessories used creatively to add beauty and interest to the table setting. In particular, figurines and other objects are often used in conjunction with the floral designs.

Candles are often attractive additions to table settings, both in the home and at the flower show. In flower shows, candles are permitted on all tables. Many etiquette and table setting books will say that candles should be used only on dinner tables, or if used in the daytime, it should be only for special occasions, such as holidays, weddings, anniversary tables, etc. Their use is permitted on flower show tables whenever the exhibitor chooses and feels they are appropriate, adding to the quality and distinction of the table, since these tables are artistic exhibits meant to emphasize choice and compatibility of components. Occasionally there is discussion about whether candles are to be classified as accessories or some other type of component. The HANDBOOK FOR FLOWER SHOWS defines components as being either plant materials, container, base, accessory(s), feature, mechanics or special staging. Since candles are not singled out in that definition as having some unique and special status, they could fit into no other category except that of being an accessory, or possibly a feature.

If used on an actual dining table or on a Functional table in a flower show, candles should be of an adequate height so that diners would not be looking directly into the flame. This is very uncomfortable, and your first aim in setting any dining table is always directed toward the comfort and enjoyment of the diners. Of course, for safety reasons, candles on flower show tables are never actually lit. It is not required that wicks be charred.

Candlesticks and candelabra are made of every imaginable material, so there is a suitable one for every possible table setting. The style, or design, and the material from which they are made will govern suitability and use of these objects.

When candles are used, they should be firmly fixed into their holders so there is no leaning or wobbling. This is an aesthetic necessity as well as a safety requirement. Candle "grips" are sold commercially, and every flower arranger should have such things as floral clay and floral tape in his or her tool kit. These may be used either to make the candle-end larger in the case of the tape, or to anchor the candle in the holder by use of the clay. Another solution is to either dip the candle's

Fig. 9 shows a wide variety of candlesticks and candelabra, ranging from the very impressive multi-branched bronze candelabrum to the sleek contemporary metal and wood ones, as well as the whimsical one with a brass sun face.

end into very hot water so that the wax softens, allowing the candle to be firmly wedged into the holder; or to apply a burning match to soften the candle-end in order to drip some hot wax into the holder. As the wax hardens, it will hold the candle firmly. If a candle is too large, it can be trimmed to fit the candlestick's socket by using a sharp knife whose blade has been heated. This will prevent the candle from splintering when it is cut. To impale a candle onto a candlestick which has a heavy spike, heat the spike first so the candle will not split.

Candles are available today in almost every possible color, but it is sometimes hard to find exactly the shade we want. Candles can be tinted or colored to meet your color needs. Pastel chalk can be used, applying it directly to the candle, then rubbing gently with a piece of soft fabric or a cotton ball to blend. Candles can be colored with lipsticks and eye shadows, again blending with a soft piece of cloth – not cotton balls in this case, since it would adhere to the lipstick. Candles can also be painted with spray paints, but these cannot be burned. Candles treated by the other methods can be burned.

Setting The Table

In general, we may state certain rules or guidelines which will be true in setting any table for any occasion: the plate and the flatware should be placed about one inch from the table edge, with forks to the left of the plate, knives and spoons to the right of the plate. Knives are always placed with their cutting edges toward the plate. The exception will be butter knives or spreaders, which are placed on the bread and butter plate either parallel to the table's edge or diagonally across one side. Whatever the menu, even for the most formal of meals, no more than three forks or knives should be placed on the table at any one time. If more are needed, they are brought in as the course requiring them is served. Except for family meals, dessert flatware is usually brought in with the dessert service. For informal family meals, these utensils may be placed on the table with all other needed flatware. All these utensils are arranged in the order in which they will be used, moving from the outside in towards the plate. Water glasses are placed above the tip of the knife, and any other glasses needed are then placed to the right of the water glass, slightly down toward the table edge in descending order in which they will be used. If three glasses are used, they are usually placed in a triangle. If more than three are used, they will be added at the time they are needed in order to avoid over-crowding. The following diagrams illustrate placement of appointments for setting a table correctly.

ABOVE — SETTING FOR BREAKFAST

1 – Cereal Bowl
2 – Plate
3 – Bread and Butter Plate
4 – Water Glass (if desired)
5 – Juice Glass
6 – Cup and Saucer

A – Napkin
B – Butter Spreader
C – Fork
D – Knife.
E – Cereal Spoon (soup spoon is used for cereal)
F – Spoon for Coffee or Tea

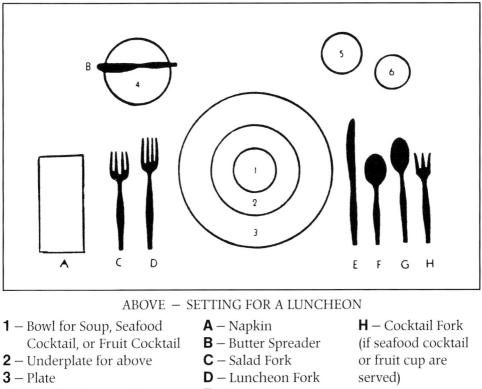

ABOVE — SETTING FOR A LUNCHEON

1 – Bowl for Soup, Seafood
    Cocktail, or Fruit Cocktail
2 – Underplate for above
3 – Plate
4 – Bread and Butter Plate
5 – Water Glass
6 – Iced Tea Glass

A – Napkin
B – Butter Spreader
C – Salad Fork
D – Luncheon Fork
E – Knife
F – Soup Spoon
G – Iced Tea Spoon

H – Cocktail Fork
(if seafood cocktail
or fruit cup are
served)

The coffee spoon will be placed when coffee is served.

The salad plate is not in place since it would be served after the soup or cocktail. If served as a separate course, it would be placed on the plate after removal of the soup or cocktail course. If served with the main course, it would be placed where the bread and butter plate is in the diagram, with the bread and butter plate placed to the left of the salad plate, and down at an angle from it, toward the direction of the table edge.

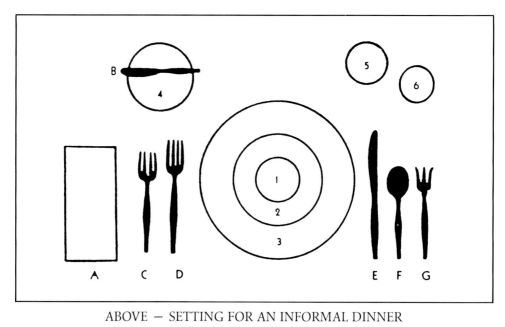

ABOVE — SETTING FOR AN INFORMAL DINNER

1 – Bowl for Soup, Seafood
Cocktail, or Fruit Cocktail
2 – Underplate for above
3 – Plate
4 – Bread and Butter Plate
5 – Water Glass
6 – Wine Glass

A – Napkin
B – Butter Spreader
C – Salad Fork
D – Dinner Fork
E – Knife
F – Soup Spoon

G – Seafood Fork
(in place if soup is
not served); OR
Cocktail Spoon
(if fruit cocktail
is served)

The coffee spoon is not in place since it would placed when coffee is served.

The salad plate is not in place. If it is served as a separate course, it would be placed on the plate after the soup or cocktail bowl had been removed. If it is served with the main course, it would be placed where the bread and butter plate is in the diagram, with the bread and butter plate placed to the left of the salad plate, and down at an angle toward the table edge.

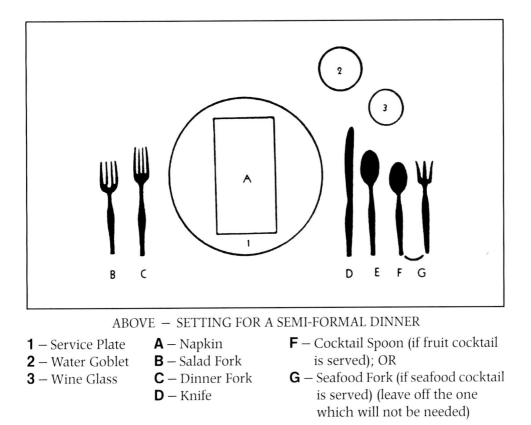

ABOVE — SETTING FOR A SEMI-FORMAL DINNER

1 – Service Plate   **A** – Napkin   **F** – Cocktail Spoon (if fruit cocktail
2 – Water Goblet   **B** – Salad Fork   is served); OR
3 – Wine Glass   **C** – Dinner Fork   **G** – Seafood Fork (if seafood cocktail
                  D – Knife   is served) (leave off the one
                                          which will not be needed)

The coffee spoon and dessert silver are not in place since they would placed when these are served.

No salad plate is shown, since it would be placed on the service plate as a separate course, and would be removed before the next course would be served.

It should be stated that all tables are set first and foremost in a manner which allows comfort and convenience for all diners. Beauty is essential, but it is secondary to the smooth and comfortable service of the meal.

CHAPTER 3.
CENTER STAGE: THE DECORATIVE UNIT

For most of us, our first interest in flower arranging was probably inspired by the desire to make an attractive arrangement for our dining table. Perhaps all of the family was coming for a holiday meal, or the boss was coming for dinner, or a group of friends were invited for a bridge luncheon. I'm sure everyone can recall those first efforts. Usually at the last minute, after the table had been set, we thought , "There should be flowers on the table!". This probably inspired a mad dash into the garden to look for whatever might be in bloom, or to the supermarket for one of those little "mixed bouquets". Then the tightly clutched bunch of plant materials would be plunked into a vase or other container without much attention to design, or to the conditioning of the materials to assure that they would at least last for the duration of the meal without wilting, or to mechanics, since we had little knowledge of any of these things. If you are at that stage now, don't despair – these things can be learned relatively easily (and fairly painlessly!). If through study you have gained more skills, each of us can always learn *more*, so our flower arrangements will give great pleasure to us as well as to our family and guests.

Perhaps the "centerpiece" for your table settings at times is simply one lovely flower in a bud vase or an especially attractive plant growing in a pot. For use in your own home, these are perfectly acceptable, and who among us has not resorted to such quick solutions at times? Living plant material does add that special "touch of life" which we all enjoy on our dining tables. A bowl of fresh fruit or one of colorful vegetables would be a colorful and long-lasting alternative to those other more simplistic ways of having some attractive plant materials on your table. Some interesting leaves, with their stems placed in water-filled tubes to keep them fresh, would be attractive additions to the fruits and/or vegetables to give variety of form, color and texture.

In a flower show, of course, using just a flower in a bud vase or a container-grown plant would not be permitted, since an *arrangement* of plant materials (with or without other components) is required. This is true of all table settings classes in flower shows, except in those classes specifying Exhibition Table Settings, Type II. In these Type II table settings, there is no completed arrangement present – plant materials are simply used to supply needed color, texture and balance to the overall design, and to show the coordination of all components.

Living plants with exposed roots may be used in flower shows, such plants as well-scrubbed scallions, for example, or for practical reasons, those plants such as bromeliads which you would like to repot after using them in a design. If the roots of any chosen plants add nothing positive to the design, these would probably be hidden from view for aesthetic reasons. If the exposed roots *do* add interest to the design, however, then they may be visible if the designer wishes. Moss may also be used, if desired, but the incorporation of plants growing in containers into designs is not allowed in flower shows.

What Is a Decorative Unit?

There are many descriptive words often used to designate the same thing. Many refer to the arrangement used on a dining table as the "centerpiece". This word is not always accurate, since the arrangement may not always be placed in the center of the table. Placement of the flower arrangement on the table will be determined by how the need for balance and better proportion to the overall design can best be met, and also by the type of meal planned.

You might consider having two arrangements on the table, one for each half of the table, rather than just one in the center. An arrangement on a buffet table, tea table, or reception table may often be seen to its best advantage if it is placed to the back or to one side of the table, rather than in the center of it. This placement might also be needed to give a more pleasing visual balance to the table.

This word usage ("centerpiece") is a common example of a term which had a definite meaning when it first came to be used, but no longer is always precisely correct. Others may refer to the arrangement on a table as "the design" or "floral design". THE HANDBOOK FOR FLOWER SHOWS uses the term, decorative unit, to refer to the arrangement of plant materials which is used on a table . The decorative unit may also include such other components as candles, as well as other accessories (such as figurines, wood carvings, seashells, and an infinite number of other things which are considered to be accessories) in addition to the arrangement of plant materials, if desired. We may all use whatever we like within the limits of good taste on table settings in our homes. In flower shows, we are permitted to use accessories and/or features unless otherwise specified in the show's schedule

Suitability To the Occasion and Other Components

If it seems that the words "suitability and compatibility" are being used over and over in this book, they *are*, for the simple reason that these are the keys to beautiful, harmonious and successful table settings. In your own home and in flower shows, the type of meal to be served and the setting in which it will be served will dictate what kind of appointments/components will be chosen and what kind of decorative unit would be best-suited to those appointments. In the home, the setting will be *actual*, while in the flower show, it is *contrived*, so the schedule will indicate what the degree of formality should be, and this will determine what style of decorative unit will be needed to complement the table as a whole. The exhibitor will know this by the class title as well as by the class's description and statement of requirements.

For example, for a class titled "Backyard Barbecue", you would not place a delicate traditional Mass design of sweet peas and roses in delicate pastel shades, arranged in a fine china container, on a tablecloth of coarsely woven stripes with settings of brightly-colored plastic dishes. Your own good taste would tell you that textures, as well as the *style* of the decorative unit were wrong for the other components and for the occasion. You would know that the decorative unit for this particular table should be of more coarsely textured, brighter colored plant materials, that these should be arranged in a much more casual and informal manner, and in a more suitable container.

The same guidelines would apply for a table setting in the home. The style of the decorative unit should always be in harmony with the table appointments with which it is to be used, as well as the room in which it will be placed. In other words, a generalized statement can be made that highly-stylized creative designs or abstract designs would not be suited to a formal, traditional room setting with its appropriate accompanying appointments. Vice versa, a traditional Mass design of soft colors would not be a good choice of design-style for a casual meal in the kitchen, on a table which is set with heavy pottery appointments in bright or earthy colors and rough textures.

Another decision which must be made when planning a decorative unit concerns where it will be placed on the table. This will be determined to some extent by the type of meal to be served. For example, most seated meals require a fairly low design, which allows guests to see over it and converse easily. Conversation is one of the most enjoyable aspects of any meal, and no one will thank you if they are constantly forced to lean sideways or rise in their chair in order to see the person across the table from them. Another approach might be to use a very tall design, which enables people to see across the table by looking under it. It should be tall enough that people don't have to bend over in order to see under it.

An arrangement for a buffet table, a tea table or a reception table can be much taller, if desired, since no one will be seated at these tables. The whole point in serving a meal buffet style is to entertain more people than you would be able to serve for a seated meal. If your floral arrangement for such an occasion is a low one of the type you would probably use for a seated meal, remember that there will be many people standing in the room at one time, and a low arrangement will be lost from view. Buffet meals are the perfect occasion to create a tall, dramatic design. It will be easily seen, and also gives your guests something to talk about if all other topics for conversation have been exhausted! For a buffet table, as well as for every other kind of table, ease of service and comfort of your guests are always important. That large arrangement would be fine if the buffet table is to be placed against a wall and all food service is to be from the front of the table. If guests are serving themselves from both sides of the table, however, then special care and planning must be given to assure that the arrangement is sturdy and stable, and does not interfere with the service of food.

The proportion and scale of the decorative unit to the overall table setting must be considered. Generally speaking, the decorative unit should occupy no less than one-fourth of the table's surface, and no more than one-third. It is very important that those eating at the table do not feel too crowded or overwhelmed by the decorative unit.

Achieving Creativity and Distinction

Creativity can be achieved in a decorative unit in several ways: by using unusual materials or creative combination of materials; through use of color and unexpected color combinations; by unexpected placement on the table; through the choice of interesting containers and/or other staging devices; by using ordinary things in unordinary ways; and through the use of accessories. In design, there are always many different routes to the same destination. The only restricting factors will be whether what is done or used is in good taste, and if it contributes to (and *never* interferes with) comfortable and pleasant dining.

Do not confuse creativity, which is synonymous with originality and uniqueness, with distinction. We should expect all of our dining tables, whether they are for our homes or for exhibition in a flower show, to have distinction. THE HANDBOOK FOR FLOWER SHOWS defines distinction as "marked superiority in all respects". Many things would be considered when evaluating a table setting for distinctiveness: the techniques and skills of the designer and the condition of all components are important considerations. In the decorative unit, this would mean that it is carefully put together, with the mechanics not too visible or distracting. The container, base and accessories, if used, should be clean and free from chips, cracks, smudges or any other unattractive marring. The plant materials should be clean, free from insect damage or spray residue, and should be fresh, crisp and well-conditioned. The same high standard for impeccability would be applied to all components used for a table setting. We always expect everything used on a dining table to be immaculate.

Selecting Plant Materials

Special attention must be paid to the selection of plant materials for the decorative units of table settings. Those flowers with especially strong fragrances, such as gardenias, sweet peas, etc., may be too over-powering for some people, and may compete with the appealing aroma of food. Others, such as marigolds, have a strong odor, which many people find unpleasant, so you might not want to include them on a dining table. When we stop to think about it, there are a number of different characteristics of plant materials which we need to consider other than just whether they are the right color, form, size and texture.

If you have a garden, you can always have some kind of plant materials available for use on your table. Don't give up just because you went into your garden and found very little in bloom there. Look at all of your trees and shrubs, seeking branches with interesting and attractive lines or curves. These can be found whether the plants are in the delicate leaf of spring, the full leaf of summer, the exciting coloring of autumn, or when they are bare in winter. At all stages, they are beautiful. Cut some of these for the main lines of your arrangement.

Continue examining the foliages of your shrubs, the plants in your flower borders, as well as those of your house plants. You will find a number of lovely leaves in varied shades of green, white, red, rust, purple and gray, as well as a number of other color possibilities. They will be of differing forms and textures as well. Cut selectively, so that you have enough variety for contrasted interest in your arrangement, but not so much that there will be confusion within the design because of the use of too many different kinds of materials. After conditioning them so they will last as long as possible, make an arrangement with just these foliages you have gathered. You may be surprised to see how lovely this can be.

We don't always want arrangements of just foliages, however, so if you do have a garden, when you plant it you should plan to include a number of flowers in colors, forms, and textures which will complement the table setting appointments you own, as well as their room-settings.

When you cut flowers from your garden, your arrangements will be much more interesting if you can include flowers at varying stages of maturity. In other words, choose some that are still in bud, others that are just partially open, and still others that are fully open. This will give variety in size, form, and in some cases, variation in color and pattern to your designs. Many plants also have very interesting seed pods which may be cut when they are green for use in fresh arrangements, or be allowed to dry for use in more rustic or casual decorative units.

If all else fails, go to the florist and select some flowers which are compatible with the appointments you plan to use. It is possible to "stretch" just a few purchased flowers into an attractive arrangement by combining your few fresh flowers with some dried line materials and some dried "filler" materials, or with branches and foliages from your garden.

At those times when you want to buy a greater number of flowers for use in a spectacular large arrangement for a buffet or reception table, or for a traditional Mass design incorporating a variety of different forms and tints, shades and tones of colors, be just as selective — if not *more* so — of the materials that you buy.

When you buy flowers, choose them carefully. Look at the back of each flower: if you see petals that are broken, shriveled, dropping off, then that particular flower is past its prime for freshness and will soon wilt and die. Look at the foliage: if the leaves are dried, rotting, and in generally bad condition, that is another indication that the flower has been in storage for a long time and is almost ready to die. Don't buy flowers like these. Explain to your florist why you don't want them — he needs to be aware that his customers understand the difference between fresh flowers and those in poor condition — and tell him you would like fresher flowers. If none are available, go to another store to buy what you need.

As in flowers that are cut from the garden, when you buy flowers from the florist try to select some in varying stages of development. This will be much more difficult to do, since most flowers are cut in bud for shipment and most will be at the same degree of openness when you see them at the florist's shop. However, if you look carefully you may find some buds, or at least some variation in sizes of the flowers, even if it is slight. These variations will make your arrangements more interesting than they would be if all plant materials in the design were uniform in size and at the same degree of openness.

Don't forget the tremendous possibilities of fruits and/or vegetables for use in designs. They have exciting variations in form, as well as in color and texture. They will be found in great variety in every good supermarket or produce market, and they are inexpensive alternatives to flowers for use in arrangements. Fruits and vegetables do not have to be used only with rough-textured, very casual appointments, either. Some of the very smooth, satiny fruits which look as if they have been polished to a high degree can be very compatible with appointments of a higher quality.

Whatever plant materials you use, be sure that you choose those which are compatible in color, texture, form and scale to the table appointments with which they are to be used, and also that they are clean and well-conditioned.

Grooming and Conditioning of Plant Materials

Grooming is the term used to describe anything which we do to plant materials to make them more attractive, such as cleaning, pruning and reshaping, or the removal of dead or damaged leaves and petals, insect damage, spray residue, etc. You may do whatever you like in this vein to plant materials for use in your own home, but in a flower show there are some limits to what you should do. Generally speaking, it is a good guideline to keep in mind that in most instances you should not groom to the extent that the true and typical form of any flower or other plant material is lost. In meeting design requirements for plant materials to be used in abstract designs, however, plant material may be abstracted or changed as needed for use in these designs. Even then, there should never be the appearance of mutilation.

Also you may never polish foliage with any commercial "leaf-shine" product, milk, oils, or any other such substance. An attractive, clean sheen can be obtained by burnishing a leaf with a piece of old nylon stocking, and this is perfectly legal. You may also use a soft artist's brush to clean plant material. It is possible to force a bloom into a more attractive stage of openness by working around inside the flower with this brush, taking care not to break a petal or stamens.

One requirement is that no color of any kind can ever be used on fresh plant materials exhibited in flower shows. This applies not only to garden-grown materials, but also to those materials purchased from florists. The only exception is that a slight amount of embellishment of fresh foliage may be allowed by the schedule in a holiday show. Embellishment is the addition of "artificial snow" or glitter, etc. to fresh greens or dried plant materials in a holiday show. The schedule must state if this is to be allowed. Dried plant materials may be treated in these, as well as in other ways, such as painting, tinting, etc., if the schedule permits.

Conditioning is a term used to describe the treatment given to plant materials to make them stay fresh for a longer time. Basically, what needs to be done to preserve plant materials in good condition for the longest time is:

(1) Cut plant materials in early morning or late afternoon when the greatest amount of moisture and sugar will be present in them. Never cut in the hottest part of the day.

(2) Take a clean bucket filled with cool-to-tepid water into the garden with you. As

soon as any plant material is cut, it should be placed into the water immediately. Stems should be cut on a slant so the stem end does not rest squarely on the bottom of the bucket, cutting off the intake of water. A sharp knife or shears should be used so that a neat, clean cut is made without crushing the stem. You may then make a second cut to the stem while holding it underwater, so there will be no trapped air bubbles in the stem to cut off the flow of water. This second cut should also be a slanting one.

(3) Heavy stems should be split to allow greater intake of water. Very heavy stems should also have the bark peeled away for an inch or more, or else should be gently pounded with a hammer, which will allow more water to be absorbed.

(4) Leaves which would be underwater should be removed since they will decay and contaminate the water. Don't remove all leaves, of course, since your design would be unattractive without any leaves. Just be sure that the water level is not so high that all leaves are underwater.

(5) After cutting, the bucket of plant materials should be placed in a cool, dark, draft-free place for several hours. Overnight is much better if it is possible.

(6) Foliages which are difficult to condition will benefit from being submerged or floated for several hours in a bathtub filled with cool water. This is also true of anthuriums, which absorb water much more readily through the surface of the flower than through the stem. Foliages with gray leaves or those with a felted surface should not be submerged or floated, since these textured surfaces will be damaged and the entire leaf will usually become very limp.

(7) Some flowers need special treatment. Those which have a milky sap, such as poinsettias and other members of the euphorbia family, poppies and dahlias, need to have the ends of their stems seared in order to stop the flow of this sap. Otherwise, it will seal the cut-end of the stem as the sap finally starts to coagulate, and this will stop the flow of water to the flower head and leaves. The searing can be done with a lighted match or candle, with a cigarette lighter, or on the hot elements of your kitchen range. Those hollow-stemmed flowers, such as delphiniums, should be filled with water after cutting. Place your finger over the cut end and place it into the bucket, so water will remain in the stem.

(8) Florist flowers will also last much longer if they are given the same treatment described above. Cut off about an inch from the bottom of the stem, and then follow the same conditioning procedure as for garden-grown materials.

Containers: "Store-bought" and "Home-made"

A container is any receptacle for plant material. If fresh plant materials are to be used, the container must be one which will hold water, or else some other provision must be made for holding the needed water. Using another container within the container which cannot hold the required moisture is one solution.

Because containers become such an important, integral part of the overall floral design, they must be well-suited to the plant materials placed within them as well as to the table setting and the room setting in which they are placed. Types and styles of containers vary greatly. They may be made of a wide variety of materials, ranging from fine china and porcelain to heavy ceramic or pottery. Metal, plastic, glass, stone, marble, basketry, wood, or alabaster are other possibilities. (Alabaster containers will be severely damaged if water is put directly into them, since water will cause the alabaster to split and crumble. Another container can be placed inside it, being careful not to allow any water to spill into the alabaster one, or the alabaster container can be protected by pouring warm — not extremely hot — melted wax into it and gently swirling the wax around to completely coat the inside surface of the container.)

Containers are found in many different shapes as well. They may be shallow bowls or other shallow containers with such shapes as rectangles, triangles, etc.; also there are cylinders, urns, goblets, chalices, compotes, pedestaled ones, pillars, jugs, or the free-form (non-geometric) ones and very imaginative ones having numerous openings, which are made to be used for creative or abstract designs. The style or type of arrangement you plan to make must be pre-determined in order to create a decorative unit which will be in harmony with the table appointments and the occasion. This, in turn, will determine what kind of container you will choose.

Colors of containers are just as widely varied. They are often found in neutral colors, such as white, black or gray. These colors can be very attractive when combined with flowers, but you will find that both black and white containers may become too dominant in the design unless the plant materials to be placed in them are carefully chosen. Usually a white container will be used most successfully if there is a fair amount of white plant material incorporated into the arrangement. Black containers are dramatic, and will need to be used with carefully chosen colors, or else the arrangement itself must be large or dynamic enough that it is capable of holding its own with the potentially dominant container. Gray containers combine well with most colors of plant materials, and do not demand a great deal of attention for themselves unless they are exceptionally large and dramatic in style.

Subdued colors, such as green, beige, and tan go well with most colors of plant materials and are not excessively attention-demanding, unless they are very large and dramatic in form, style and in texture. Brilliant, pure-colored containers are best used with plant materials in their same color-family so that together they all combine into a harmonious, well-related color harmony. Pastel containers, by the same token, are best used with tints, shades and tones of the same colors of plant materials as that of the container.

Usually matte-finished containers are easier to work with than are bright, shiny ones, and plain ones are less distractive than highly patterned ones. There can be no general statement made, however, that one kind of container is preferable over other kinds. The determining factor will be the style of design and the kinds of plant materials you plan to place in it, as well as its suitability and compatibility with other components used in the table setting.

Our grandmothers required that all such containers be "vases" in the truest and most literal sense of the word, and it would have been a rare exception to see flowers placed in any other kind of container than an actual " vase". Only the most daring and innovative woman would have thought of doing such a thing, and she would have been considered very odd, indeed, by her friends and neighbors! Today, anything which is compatible with other appointments may be used as a container for the decorative unit.

Every home has a wide range of possibilities in things which could be used as a container. Such things as vegetable dishes, pitchers, teapots, sugar bowls, gravy boats, and other decorative or utilitarian items never intended for use as floral containers might be chosen. Look through your cabinets and cupboards with a "new eye", evaluating all the things you own for their possible use as containers for the decorative unit on your tables. You'll be pleasantly surprised by the number of ideas you will have. The major consideration must be that the container is well-related in color and in texture to the plant materials which will be placed in it, as well as to the overall table setting which the decorative unit is meant to complement. It must be compatible in style, spirit, degree of formality, color and texture, as well as being in pleasing scale to both the plant materials and the overall design.

Many things can be easily adapted for use as containers. Florists and crafts shops often stock an item called a candle-cup adapter. This is a bowl-like object with a protrusion on the bottom which fits into the candle socket of a candlestick or candelabra. Oasis or a needlepoint holder can be placed in the bowl of the candle-cup adapter to hold the plant materials and provide moisture to keep them fresh. The adapter should be firmly attached to the candlestick by putting floral clay around the part of the adapter which fits into the candleholder, and then after the Oasis is put in, it should be taped to the bowl of the adapter with floral tape so that the finished arrangement does not wobble or fall over. A wine bottle or any other type of bottle or jug could also be used in the same manner.

A glass or plastic bowl might be placed in a basket or a wooden bowl to hold the plant materials for a decorative unit. Every craft and gift shop is filled with attractive baskets from all over the world, and they lend themselves beautifully to use on many informal table settings. Wooden containers also are very compatible with many informal appointments. Arrangements should never be made directly in wooden containers, since contact with moisture may cause the wood to split.

Attractive containers can be made from many objects found in your local hardware or builder's supply store. PVC pipe can be used to make very contemporary-looking containers. This is done by cutting the pipe into varying lengths and gluing them together into a single unit, or the cut pipes can also be combined with interestingly shaped pieces cut from wood. (Please refer to the yellow and the black ones seen on the lower level in Fig. 10 to see two which were made in the manner just described.) These kinds of containers can be painted any color you wish. Holes or openings can also be cut into the pipes wherever you like, so that plant materials can emerge at varied angles and placements. Cans, bottles, or wet Oasis in plastic bags can be used inside these bottomless pipes to keep plant materials fresh.

For use in more traditional designs, newel posts for stairs or old chair legs with plastic bowls glued to their tops can be painted in any desired color to make attractive containers. A base should be attached to these containers for better visual balance and for actual stability. Any color found in nature can be found or created on containers by applying various kinds of coatings, as well as by painting, staining, or by some other means of applying color to surfaces.

Metal or plastic drainpipes can be made into unusual containers with nails or glue, paint and a wooden base. These may be either plain, fluted, or corrugated and of several different shapes — round, square, or rectangular. Metal ones can have a piece of copper cut to fit, which can then be soldered into the bottom of the pipe to make it water-tight. Push this piece up into the pipe for a short distance before soldering it in place so that it will not be visible. After cleaning and sanding, the pipe container can be painted any color you like. The addition of a slightly larger wooden base, painted the same color, will make the container look more balanced.

Tall juice cans can be used alone, or more than one can be stacked and glued together, then covered with such things as marbleized paper; thin wood veneer sheets; sheets of copper or brass which can be found at many craft supply stores; rope or heavy twine wound round and round it, then glued into place; or the materials sold at many craft supply stores to cane chair seats are a few possibilities.

Fig. 10 shows a selection of containers which would be suitable on a wide variety of tables. The pewter candle mold on the back row, the blue salt-glazed crock, and the copper mug and casserole on the bottom row would be very much at home in a casual or Early American setting. The pink fish pitcher and the green cabbage sauce boat are examples of things found in the kitchen which would be very attractive in an informal setting. The spiraling brass candlestick shows a candle-cup adapter next to it, which would convert the candlestick into a container. The silver Grecian figure holding an iridescent bowl and the pierced china bowl next to it would be compatible to a more formal, elegant setting. The three containers on the bottom row are examples of hand-crafted containers: the yellow one is of differing lengths of PVC pipes glued together and then painted; a brown cane-covered can is in the center of the group; the contemporary black container is of sawed wood pieces, with holes drilled to hold two upright pieces of PVC pipes. The whole is then painted black. The bright red, circular container and the gray columnar one would be well-suited to more contemporary tables.

A sheet of plumbers' lead can be bought at a plumbers' supply store or at many builders' supply stores. It can have its edges turned up to the desired height and then can be formed into any geometric or free-form shape which pleases you. The final result will be a container which looks like pewter.

Look for unusual containers, or things that can be adapted for use as containers at garage sales, junk shops and antiques shops, and even at the grocery market. Such things supplied by Mother Nature as shells, minerals, coconut shells or pieces of cleaned decorative wood also make lovely containers when used with compatible appointments and room settings.

Bases

A base is anything used underneath a flower arrangement, or decorative unit, such as a stand, mat, burl or slice of wood, piece of cork, etc. Bases may be formal and traditional in feeling or they may be rustic and casual. The style, character, color and texture of a base must be carefully chosen, so that it is in keeping with the decorative unit with which it is used, and with the other table setting components as well.

There are many lovely kinds of bases which are made for the purpose, and they may be purchased for use with flower arrangements. The Japanese and Chinese manufacture many beautiful stands and bases in a wide variety of sizes and styles. Many of them are exquisitely carved, so they are works of art within themselves. When using bases of this type, the designer must take care that they are compatible with the arrangement, and also that the base does not become the most dominant component within the design.

Other bases of more formal character are those of marble, found also in many different sizes, colors, and shapes. If you are trying to build a collection of bases, and would like to have some marble ones, look in the housewares section of local department stores as well as in those shops selling gifts and imported wares. You can often find lovely marble pieces which were made for use as serving pieces, such as cheese boards, trivets, etc. They may not have been created by their makers for use with flower arrangements, but they serve that purpose very well. You can also buy squares of marble in many different colors at building-supply stores or those selling tiles. Glue some felt pieces to the bottom of these tiles to prevent the marring of your furniture, and you will have a beautiful base for your designs.

Many wooden bases and stands can be found in stores. These may also have been made for use in the service of food, but they lend themselves well to use as bases. Circles and rectangles of cork, made for use as trivets to protect tables from hot dishes can also be found, and they are well adapted for use as bases with informal decorative units.

Wooden bases can be cut from boards or plywood into any shape you wish, then stained or painted to fulfill any particular need. Craft supply stores also often stock irregularly shaped pieces of wood: these are usually being offered for use in making a type of clock, with numbers and hands intended to be mounted onto the face of the wood, but they make wonderful bases. In these same kinds of stores you can find beveled circular, oval or rectangular shapes of unfinished wood in various sizes. These can be sanded, then painted or stained in any color you like to create very attractive bases.

The reason for using a base may vary with the particular design. A base can give a design more importance by elevating it. Bases may be used to protect the table's surface. They may be used for the beauty and interest they contribute to the design and to the setting, and they may aid the overall balance of the design, depending on where the arrangement is placed upon it.

Techniques and Mechanics of Flower Arranging

Mechanics are contrivances used to hold and control plant materials in designs. A good "rule" is that mechanics should always be as invisible and unobtrusive as you can make them. As you work with arranging flowers, you will acquire more and more techniques for dealing with many situations.

There are certain tools and aids available commercially for the arranging of flowers. One is called a needlepoint holder. The Japanese call them kenzans. They are also known as pinholders, and consist of rows or circles of sharply pointed metal pins, embedded into metal or plastic. If at all possible, you should invest in lead-based ones. The plastic ones are too lightweight to be really useful and they do not last very long. Needlepoint holders are available in a wide variety of shapes and sizes. If you become much interested in flower arranging, you will want a good selection of these.

You should choose the smallest possible size of needlepoint holder which is able to hold all of the stems of plant materials to be used in a particular design. Otherwise, it will be necessary to find some means of concealing the holder after the design is finished. On the other hand, avoid trying to cram too large a quantity of materials onto a too-small needlepoint holder. This will cause all of the stems to be forced into a rigidly upright position, destroying the grace of the design. Also, if the outer stems are barely stuck onto the pins, those stems will be constantly falling over. It can be embarrassing if your flower arrangement begins to fall apart before the eyes of your guests!

Some very attractive polished stones, as well as clear or colored glass cullets are available for the purpose of hiding mechanics, but for a more professional and "finished" look to your designs, you should avoid resorting to excessive use of these types of things for hiding mechanics. Ideally, these aids should be used only when they add to the attractiveness of the design by contributing needed color, texture, or variation in forms, rather than for hiding mechanics. The worst solution of all is a collar of leaves surrounding the base of the design, obvious to one and all that the primary purpose is to hide a needleholder. To make needlepoint holders as inconspicuous as possible, they can be painted the same color as the container.

There are also lead cupholders, which have needlepoint holders attached in them. These are used in designs in which a container is not used, such as on a base with fruits, vegetables and/or flowers and foliages. They may also be used in containers which do not hold water, such as baskets, wooden pieces, PVC pipes, or decorative wood. These, too, can be painted the same color as a base or container so they will blend into the design and not call undue attention to themselves.

It is highly recommended that a special tool kit be assembled for use in arranging flowers. If you are interested in competition in flower shows or in presenting programs on flower arranging, you would be wise to gather your needed tools and aids in a portable basket, a tool box or a fishing equipment box. In my own kit, I have the following items: wire in various lengths and gauges; floral tapes in brown, black, green and white (other colors are available, these are simply the ones I find most useful); floral clay; wooden meat or hors-d'oeuvre skewers of various lengths, to be used for lengthening or strengthening stems (these are sold at your grocery store, in the housewares section of department stores, at kitchen-ware stores, etc.); scissors; pruning shears, or other sharp shears; pins; toothpicks; both Scotch and masking tapes; plastic tubes to hold water for short-stemmed materials; a knife for cutting Oasis or other foam materials; special floral tape which is used to attach Oasis firmly to a container; a glue gun and glue sticks for the gun; and various other things from time to time which I might find to be helpful. An arranger's tool kit is very personalized and should contain everything possible to help in putting together an arrangement attractively and securely. If you are assembling tools and aids together in one spot to make arrangements for the home, perhaps a kitchen drawer could be spared for this purpose. A good collection of tools and aids for mechanics are just as important for the arranger who only wishes to do flower arrangements for the home, as it is for those who are interested in competing in flower shows.

When using a needlepoint holder in a container, it should be firmly attached to the container. To do this, make a coil of floral clay long enough to go around the outer circumference of the needlepoint holder. This is done by rolling the clay between the hands to soften and lengthen it. Attach the clay around the outer edge of the holder by pressing it. The clay should be placed about a quarter-inch in from the holder's edge. Press it down firmly in the container, while at the same time, giving it a slight turn. This will create a good seal between the container and the needlepoint holder. In order for the clay to hold, the clay, the needlepoint and the container all must be *absolutely dry*. If any moisture is present, the seal will not hold. If your seal was not good and water has gotten underneath the holder, it will become loose and the arrangement may fall over. If this happens to you at any time, you must remove the needlepoint holder and clay from the container and begin anew after drying all parts well. Sorry, but this is the only way. Once moisture breaks the seal, no amount of pressure will ever make it hold again.

This method should not be used in a silver container because the silver will tarnish, and may be permanently discolored. It is better to anchor the needlepoint in silver containers with warm melted paraffin. You then will simply pour hot water over the paraffin to melt it when you are ready to remove the holder.

It is true that many experts in the Japanese style of flower arranging do not anchor the needlepoint into the container, believing that arrangers should be forced to perfect skills of balance in their designs. This can apply to experts, but beginners are well-advised to avoid the frustration of working with a needlepoint holder which is not firmly anchored. This is particularly important for all designs used on dining tables, those made by beginners and experts alike. Designs on table settings may be moved or bumped, causing the entire decorative unit to tip over, spilling water everywhere, and possibly damaging the table or tablecloth or breaking other components.

To use a needlepoint holder in a tall container, you will find it easier to make a pleasing design if the needlepoint holder is not at the bottom of the container. If it is placed there, that will necessitate using plant materials with much longer stems. It will also be difficult to place materials gracefully in the design since the height of the container will force all of the stems into a rigidly upright position. Instead, pour in either sand or kitty litter to within about four inches from the top of the container. Pour hot melted paraffin over the surface of the fill-material to seal it, then set a needlepoint or cupholder into the paraffin as it hardens. This will hold the needlepoint firmly in place. You will then be working nearer to the top of the container, and this will eliminate some of the afore-mentioned problems. Another possible choice of mechanics for a tall container is to use crumpled chicken wire in it, extending a few inches above the container's rim.

Oasis is the trade-name of a foam product, which absorbs many times its own weight in water, and will provide a source of moisture to plant materials whose stems are inserted into it. Oasis can be bought at florists and crafts supply stores. It is approximately the size and shape of a building brick, is green in color, and is very lightweight when dry. To use it, submerge the foam block in water until it is thoroughly saturated. It can then be cut, using a sharp knife, into any shape and sized to fit into any container.

Oasis works well for most flowers, but it should never be allowed to become dry. In order to keep the plant materials fresh, the Oasis must be completely covered by the plant materials so the foam is not exposed to the air, and ideally, it should be standing in water. Some flowers do not stay fresh over long periods when arranged in Oasis. Many roses, Gerbera daisies and most hollow-stemmed flowers, such as delphiniums, are examples. You will probably discover others which will fall into this category as you work with a wide variety of materials and gain more knowledge about them.

One distinct advantage to using Oasis is that stems can be inserted into it at angles, allowing graceful cascading placements of materials if desired. You will find that Oasis does not lend itself to "trial-and-error" arranging. As more and more holes are made in it, it will begin to crumble and you will need to start over with a new piece if this happens. Otherwise, the Oasis will split and the entire arrangement will fall apart.

Also, you must take special care if you have pulled out a stem from the arrangement for some reason, and then have replaced it into the same hole. You must replace the plant material to the exact depth that it was before. Otherwise, the stem-end will not be in contact with moisture and the materials will wilt. If fairly heavy materials are being used, you may need to give them more support by wrapping the Oasis with chicken wire to help hold the larger stems in place.

Styrofoam can be used for dried materials or for fruit and vegetable arrangements. It cannot be used with fresh materials, since it will disintegrate in water. There is a special product made for using with dried materials which is even better since it does not have holes in it, as does styrofoam, so the stems will not wobble. It is called Sahara. For making fruit and vegetable arrangements, wooden skewers are useful. Fruits can be impaled on them and then the skewer can be stuck into the styrofoam, Sahara or Oasis. Fruits which you wish to use in clusters, such as grapes, can be wired to a skewer or stick.

To anchor a piece of wood onto a needlepoint, wrap the cut end of the wood with a collar of hardware cloth which is wired tightly into place. The wire collar should extend below the base of the wood for about an inch. This wire collar can then be impaled onto a needlepoint holder, holding the wood either upright or at an angle as you wish. The wire collar gives the needlepoint something to "grab" onto, since the wood may be too hard to be impaled onto the needlepoint holder. Wood can also be nailed or screwed to another flat piece of wood or to a base to hold it firmly in place. Special needlepoint holders ,which have a hole in the center for a screw, are also made for use with decorative wood. The needlepoint is screwed into the base of the wood, with needles pointing away from the wood, and this needlepoint can then be impaled onto a second needlepoint holder, which is being used to hold all of the other plant materials.

To reinforce a weak flower stem, you may place a heavy wire or a wooden skewer along the stem and then wrap both together with floral tape, or you may insert the weak stem into another stronger, hollow stem. Always leave the cut-end of the plant material extending below the tape or the false stem so that it can take up moisture. Useful stems for this treatment are gladiolus and chrysanthemums, both of which have soft, inner parts which can be pushed out, leaving the outer stem intact, or plants which are naturally hollow.

Attention to all these details: choosing plant materials and containers which go well with each other, grooming and conditioning the plant materials carefully, and paying attention to mechanics so that your decorative unit will look well crafted — all of these things will make your decorative unit more visually appealing and will add to the enjoyment of the table setting, which is our primary goal in table settings.

The following designs would be most suited to a table setting at which no one is to be seated, or they should be placed on the table in such a way that they do not block diners' view.

Fig. 11. An opulent decorative unit for a delightful table setting. Colors and kinds of plant materials are well-related to the container, which is a pitcher from a set of matching dinnerware. The fruit motif of the pitcher is repeated by using those same fruits in the arrangement. Lines of the arrangement follow the line of the pitcher's handle, creating a very appealing and rhythmic design . The arrangement can be seen as part of a table setting in Fig. 91 (Deen Day Smith).

Fig. 12. A lovely design of autumn coloration, suitable for a buffet or reception table. The fine porcelain container has peach bands, a color which is repeated in the design of peach carnations. The dark green foliages are the same shade of green as the cloth beneath the arrangement. Contrast in color is provided by the autumn shades of the nandina foliage, rust chrysanthemums and the luscious red pears, all combined in a design of crisp, tailored appeal. (Deen Day Smith).

Fig. 13. A very appealing design with a feminine feeling. The fine porcelain container by Herend, combined with such delicately textured plant materials as eucalypyus, pink carnations, sea lavender (caspia), and tiny pink daisy chrysanthemums make this a design suitable for use on a tea table, a reception table, or even a buffet setting of compatible appointments. The overall design is light and charming. (Deen Day Smith).

Fig. 14. A bold and dramatic decorative unit, making it an ideal design for a sophisticated buffet table setting. Bare tree branches establish a highly rhythmic line structure for the arrangement, using red anthuriums and leucothe foliage. The whole is arranged in an interesting metal, two-tiered container which incorporates space in an appealing, dynamic manner. Appointments with a strongly contemporary character would be compatible with this design. (Deen Day Smith).

Fig. 15. This design has a very sculptural quality due to the plant materials used in it. Solid, patterned sansevieria establishes the main line, with large, interesting forms supplied by trimmed leeks and by differing types of vivid fresh red, green and yellow peppers. The peppers are impaled on green sticks to control their placement in the design. Aspidistra leaves furnish gracefully flowing lines, and a contrasting shade of green. The design is arranged in a cupholder on a green marble base. It would be an exciting addition to an informal, but very attractive buffet setting. (June Wood).

Fig. 16. A more traditional decorative unit which would work well on a buffet table in an informal setting. Yellow gladioli, pussy willow, yellow carnations and lilies, orange lilies and tiny, feathery yellow asters are arranged in a pewter-washed copper chalice. (June Wood).

Fig. 17. A graceful decorative unit in the traditional manner would be at home on a buffet table with compatible appointments, or on a tea or reception table. An ivory cherub container holds a flowing crescent-shaped design of purple liatris, pink and cream snapdragons, "Stargazer" lilies, Scotch broom and variegated pittosporum foliage. (June Wood).

Fig. 18. A low, flowing crescent-shaped decorative unit is composed of coralbush shrub branches, rust alstroemerias, deep garnet red chrysanthemums, with red and yellow apples. The container is a wooden compote. It is a design with a nostalgic sense of style, for use with informal components. (June Wood).

Fig. 19. A bright and cheerful decorative unit is arranged very low to enable luncheon guests to talk across it easily. Brilliant yellow Gerbera daisies are combined with dramatic variegated ginger and aralia leaves. The container is a heavy brown and green pottery bowl which has an interesting textural quality. The brown of the container repeats the large brown centers of the Gerbera daisies. An unassuming, but very pleasant design to combine with casual appointments. (June Wood).

CHAPTER 4.
LET'S CELEBRATE!
HOLIDAYS AND OTHER SPECIAL OCCASIONS

To all of us, holidays are very special days or periods in our lives — happy times which are set apart from our usual day to day routines. Holidays are days which have been given special significance — they are those dates which have been designated for religious observances, secular celebrations, commemorations of unique events in the history of a nation or group of people They are often a time to honor a person of established historical importance or one who has played a significant role in the folklore of a culture. National festivals or celebrations centering on the customs of certain national or ethnic groups enrich understanding and appreciation of those heritages. They also provide impetus for the preservation of cultural heritages.

In olden times, holidays were usually religious in character. Though we might not like to think so, many of the customs associated with some of our religious holidays had their beginnings in pagan celebrations. As the early Church attempted to convert pagans to the new religion of Christianity, some parts of pagan celebrations were often incorporated into the Christian holidays in order to lessen the importance of the ancient rites and to create different meanings about them to the new Christian converts. Many ancient religious rituals and customs have been carried over into modern times. Today, most of those adopted customs have become part of the secular celebrations of the various holidays, rather than being incorporated into religious observances.

The ancient customs often were related to events in nature, such as the annual course of the sun or phases of the moon. Many early holidays celebrated the sun's renewed warmth in spring, which allowed the planting of crops once again. Sometimes observances were held in the hope of bringing rain, and at other times, they simply offered thanksgiving for sun, rain and the abundance of crops. The very word, *holiday*, is derived from the phrase, "holy days".

Family celebrations of holidays, with the observance of each family's unique traditions, constitute some of the "mortar" which binds members of a family together. Surely for such important occasions in our lives and in those of our families, special attention should be paid to the table settings which commemorate these important family times.

New Year's

In modern-day America, for many of us New Year's calls to mind singing "Auld Lang Syne" at midnight when the New Year begins, New Year's resolutions, college football games and the Rose Parade. This holiday has many other associations connected with its celebrations, both in our own society and in others. For example, all true Southerners mark the day by eating black-eyed peas to assure good luck and money all through the year. "Superstition!", you no doubt are muttering. Maybe so, but who wants to take unnecessary risks by failing to eat that full measure of black-eyed peas? Not me, daughter of the South that I am! My family has eaten black-eyed peas on New Year's Day for as long as I can remember, and I have continued the custom in my own home, too.

In ancient Rome, Janus, the God of gates and doors as well as of beginnings and endings, was honored on the first day of the new year. Janus had two faces, one looking backward into the receding past and the other looking forward into the approaching future. He typifies our hopeful anticipation that the new year will, indeed, be better than the old one.

Early Christians celebrated New Year's Day on March 25, until the Gregorian calendar of 1582 moved it to January 1. In ancient Egypt, the New Year began in June instead of January.

The Jewish New Year, Rosh Hashanah, falls on the first and second days of the Hebrew month Tishri, in late September or early October. It is a day of solemn prayer, and begins the ten Days of Penitence which end with Yom Kippur, a day of prayer for forgiveness for the past year's sins. It is a time to pray that your name will be written into the Book of Life for the coming year.

The Chinese New Year is set by the lunar calendar and is celebrated for an entire month, beginning in late January or early February. It is a very family-orientated celebration. Everyone who is away from home returns there for the holiday if at all possible. The home is thoroughly cleaned, the entire family gets new clothes and gifts are exchanged. Peach trees in pots are forced into bloom to bring good luck in the new year. It is a time of gaiety, with fireworks, parades, Dragon dances and theatrical performances.

Many Europeans blow trumpets directed to the four corners of the world at midnight. In England, bells are rung to announce the arrival of the new year. Old "Father Time" departs for another year, and yields power to the "Baby New Year". English families also drink Wassail, which is a hot spiced tea. The word "Wassail" comes from the ancient Norse word, meaning "be healthy". A toast is made while drinking Wassail for good health in the new year.

In Scotland, visitors bring lumps of coal and a piece of bread when visiting a friend's home to assure that they will be warm and well-fed during the year. In France, pancakes cooked on a griddle are eaten for good luck, and in Spain, twelve grapes are eaten to bring twelve months of good luck.

Almost every culture has its own customs to celebrate the New Year. Perhaps your own family has special and unique ways to observe the holiday. Cherish them! They create special memories for all members of a family.

Fig. 20 shows compatible components for an elegant New Year's party. A fine cream colored and gold-rimmed china is combined with sleek, contemporary brass goblets. The tablecloth is a heavy cream brocaded linen, with a gold lamé napkin and a twisted gold napkin ring. The tall and dramatic flower arrangement would be best suited to a buffet setting. Large white lilies, with shapes reminiscent of bells, ferns and strelitzia (Bird of Paradise) leaves, clipped papyrus and lotus pods are arranged in a tall brass candlestick which has a candle-cup adapter in the top of it to hold the materials of the design. In a flower show, exhibitors are permitted to paint dried plant materials only, and then only if the schedule permits. Fresh plant material is never painted, tinted, or treated in any way, with the exception of foliages, which may have some slight embellishment for use in holiday shows if the schedule permits. (June Wood).

Fig. 21. This setting for New Year's celebration has a very contemporary feeling with well-coordinated components. Dishes shown are a gold lacquered service plate, a black plate with scalloped edge, and a salad/dessert plate of black tiger-stripes on a gold background. A brass goblet and gold coffee cup, which matches the salad/dessert plate, complete the setting. The tablecloth is a metallic gold with black stripes. A black napkin is used with a gold-banded black napkin ring. White carnations, lemon foliage, and strelitzia leaves are arranged in a square black container. Arrangers may do anything they like in arrangements made for use in *the home*. In a flower show, dried materials may be painted if the schedule permits, and there may be some embellishment of fresh foliages (but *never* flowers) in a holiday show if the schedule allows this to be done. (June Wood)

Fig. 22. A sophisticated table setting for New Year's. The stage is set by the dynamic flower arrangement, which features a spiraling Lucite sculpture mounted on a block of black plastic. The pink ginger blossoms and clipped, pink-edged dracaena are very much in keeping with the sculpture. The square black plate and slender black goblet are in the same spirit. The color of the ginger is repeated in the Majolica salad plate, the pink goblet, and the pink napkin ring. The deeper rose of the napkin is also found in the coloring of the salad plate. (June Wood)

Since the New Year's holiday comes at such a cold and dreary time of the year, it seems only fitting that those arrangements and table settings made to celebrate it should be especially cheering, carefree and glamorous, with a definite note of gaiety and exhilaration.

Valentine's Day

Saint Valentine's Day is a sentimental holiday honoring lovers. We celebrate it by sending flowers, greeting cards (Valentines) or gifts to express love and affection. This holiday is symbolized by hearts, doves (because they mate for life), Cupids, and by the colors of red and white. Cupid was a popular figure from Roman mythology, who shot people in the heart with his bow and arrow, causing them to fall in love. The holiday probably derives from the ancient Roman feast of

Lupercalis, celebrated on February 15, one day later than our present-day Valentine's Day. The festival gradually became associated with the feast day of St. Valentine, who has traditionally been regarded as the patron saint of lovers. If you are a true traditionalist, then your Valentine's dinner will include roast peacock, quails, and eggs, with figs and pomegranates for dessert. These, after all, are the foods of love so the ancient ones tell us.

Fig. 23. A very elegant and romantic setting for two features a beautiful white china with a pattern of gold fleur-de-lys, and gold-rimmed cut-glass crystal. (This spelling of fleur-de-lis is used, since the china pattern's name is "Fleur-de-lys".) Cupid holds aloft a lovely Mass design of "Stargazer" lilies, pink alstroemeria, golden acacia , golden variegated leucothoe foliage and asparagus fern (Ornamental asparagus Sprengeri). All of the components are well-suited to each other, and convey the spirit of Valentine's Day. (Deen Day Smith).

Fig. 24. Another traditional table for St. Valentine's has a somewhat more casual feeling. The white Wedgwood leaf-edged plate holds a vivid red ceramic lidded box. The box contains a Valentine's surprise of candies, or perhaps a gift. The red and white heart-shaped place mat is, in turn, patterned with stripes and hearts of varying sizes. A red napkin and red goblet complete the setting. The traditional Mass design of large red and white carnations, white mini-carnations, and green and white variegated ivy is arranged in a white Cupid container. The design is placed on a red heart-shaped base. (June Wood).

Johnny Appleseed Day

The man we have come to know as Johnny Appleseed was born in Massachusetts in 1774 or 1775. The name with which he was christened was John Chapman.

Europeans had brought apple seeds to the original eastern colonies. Johnny Appleseed is said to have taken them into the wilderness areas of western Pennsylvania and Ohio, scattering seeds as he went. He often returned to check on the resulting trees. He is believed to have traveled as far west as the Badlands of the Dakotas. He planted orchards in Michigan, Indiana, Ohio, Pennsylvania, Kentucky and Missouri.

Johnny Appleseed was also an herbalist, and he planted herbs wherever he traveled. At that time in history, herbs were the only available treatments for illnesses and injuries, so they were very important and necessary plants. Apples, too, were used for cider, vinegar, and in cooking, so they were most valuable to the early settlers.

He died on March 11, 1847, so that day is officially observed as Johnny Appleseed Day in most states. Ohio observes Johnny Appleseed Day on his birthday, and Indiana, the state where he died, has a two hundred-fifty acre park dedicated to his memory. An arrangement incorporating apples or apple-patterned dinnerware would be suitable components for a table setting to commemorate Johnny Appleseed Day.

Garden club members are modern-day seed collectors and providers. *National Council of State Garden Clubs, Inc.* observes Arbor Day to encourage the planting of trees, as well as National Garden Week to promote an interest in gardening. There is no definite date for Arbor Day, since the most appropriate time for planting trees varies due to climatic differences among the states. It is celebrated in all of the states except one on a locally-set date.

St. Patrick's Day

St. Patrick's Day is celebrated in Ireland and in the United States with great enthusiasm. The feast-day of St. Patrick occurs on March 17. Curiously enough, St. Patrick was born on March 17th and he died on the same date, March 17th. St. Patrick was Scottish, and not Irish, but the Irish enthusiastically claim him to be their own.

One symbol of the holiday is shamrocks. The shamrock (Irish Seamrog, or "Little clover") was originally chosen as the national emblem of Ireland because of the legend that St. Patrick used the plant to illustrate the Trinity. Most shamrocks, particularly the small-leafed white clover, Trifolium repens, have been considered by the Irish as good-luck charms since earliest times. This superstition has persisted into modern times among people of many nationalities. Shamrocks are worn by celebrants on St. Patrick's Day.

The celebration of St. Patrick's Day in the United States probably began in Boston in 1737. It was started by a Protestant organization called the Charitable Irish Society, which worked for the benefit of poor Irish people who were sick or in need. The Friendly Sons of St. Patrick started the celebration in Philadelphia in 1780, followed by the New York branch of the same society in 1784. The New York group was composed of both Protestant and Catholic members.

Other St. Patrick's Day symbols are Irish harps, leprechauns and the color green. Corned beef and cabbage with potatoes are traditionally eaten on this holiday, and everyone is expected to wear green clothing. The penalty for non-conformance to the tradition is a big strong pinch.

Fig. 25. This buffet table setting certainly says St. Patrick's Day. It has a subtle all-green color harmony, with the theme established by green cabbage leaf plates and serving pieces from Portugal. Green goblets and linens complete the appealing setting. The decorative unit consists of sansevieria, silver-edged ginger leaves, variegated philodendron foliages, with a cut cabbage and Brussels sprouts arranged on a round, green marble base. Using cut fruits and/or vegetables is only permitted in a flower show if the schedule specifically allows it. Of course, in your own home, you may do whatever you like, within the limits of good taste. (June Wood).

Fig. 26. A sophisticated St. Patrick's Day setting has a bold, contemporary feeling. A cabbage leaf plate is used with a black plate and goblet. The yellow-green napkin closely matches the color of the green plate and the flowers in the floral design. Swirling monkey puzzle vine is combined with yellow-green anthuriums and feathery cedar in a highly rhythmic, and inspired design. The interesting contemporary container is particularly well-suited for use in this creative design. (Deen Day Smith).

Fig. 27. Another all-green setting is highly appropriate for St. Patrick's Day. The cabbage leaf plate and a darker green service plate repeat the colors in the decorative unit. A wrought-iron container holds a two-part design of clipped umbrella palm, Bell's of Ireland (what could be a better choice?), variegated philodendron leaves, and green anthuriums. A green glass goblet and bright green napkin complete the setting for this festive occasion. (Deen Day Smith).

Easter

Easter, like many of our other holidays, is a religious observance for many and a strongly secular one for others. For Christians, Easter is the principal holy-day of the year. This annual festival, commemorating the resurrection of Jesus Christ and His triumphant victory over death, is celebrated on a Sunday of varying dates on the calendar, falling between March 22 and April 25 (on the first Sunday which follows the full moon that appears on or after the vernal equinox); therefore, this holiday is called a "moveable feast". Connected with the observance of Easter by some religious groups are the forty-days penitential season of Lent, which begins on Ash Wednesday and ends at midnight on Holy Saturday, which is the day before Easter. Holy Week begins on Palm Sunday and includes Good Friday, the day of Crucifixion. It ends on Holy Saturday, with Easter Sunday being the first day of the new week.

In early times, newly baptized Christians wore white garments. The Emperor Constantine began the tradition of the Easter parade by ordering his ministers to wear their best robes at Easter to honor Christ's resurrection. We continue this custom by wearing new clothes at Easter.

Easter, though a Christian festival, incorporates a number of pre-Christian customs. Scholars believe the name comes from Eastore, the Anglo-Saxon name of a Teutonic goddess, Ostern. She was a goddess of spring and fertility, to whom was dedicated a month corresponding to our April. The festival was celebrated on the day of the vernal equinox. Traditions associated with this festival survive in the Easter rabbit, a well known symbol of fertility, and in colored Easter eggs. These eggs were originally painted in bright colors to represent the sunshine of spring.

Giving gifts of eggs was an established custom long before the Christian era because eggs were regarded as symbols of continuing life. In ancient civilizations such as Greek, Chinese and Persian, eggs were given as gifts at spring festivals. The coloring of eggs is also a very old custom. King Edward I of England's household accounts in the year, 1290, show that eighteen pence were spent to buy four hundred and fifty eggs, which were then colored and given to members of the Royal Household. In countries of Eastern Europe, particularly in the Ukraine, elaborately painted and patterned eggs have long been a traditional peasant folk art.

Easter eggs have been an important part of American Easter celebrations as well. The first eggroll was held on the lawn of the Capitol Building, and later the event was held at the White House. Dolly Madison is credited with having begun the annual event. It was discontinued during the Civil War and during World Wars I and II. President Eisenhower reinstated the celebration in 1953. In Fredericksburg, Texas, German immigrants burned fires on the eve of Easter. They told their children that the Easter rabbit started the fires so he could make dyes from wildflowers to color the Easter eggs.

Shrovetide is the English name for the last three or four days before the start of Lent. It is a time celebrated with games, sports, dances and feasts before the beginning of Lent. In Scotland, it is called Fasten's E'en (Eve of the Fast); in France and the U.S., it is called Mardi Gras. Parts of Latin America celebrate Carnival with

Fig. 28a. This charming table setting has an air of spring due to its use of pastel flowers and appointments. The china has a motif of spring flowers — daffodils, tulips and Dutch iris — around its rim. A bright rose, lacy straw place mat, soft pink napkin and goblet complete the setting. Two Easter Bunnies, male and female, flank a lovely Mass arrangement of yellow lilies, pussy willow, blue Dutch iris, pink tulips, pink and rose alstroemeria, and pink mini-carnations. They are arranged in a shallow bowl, which is placed on pink, blue and yellow bases of graduated sizes. (June Wood).

Fig. 28b. Shows a close-up view of the china which is used in the table setting seen in Fig. 28a.

lavish costumes and parades. This is a time for freedom from rules and for exuberant celebrations.

Easter is a holy day for Christians, and it is also a day for children to enjoy the other customs, such as Easter baskets, presents from the Easter Bunny, and Easter egg hunts. Flowers associated with Easter are the Easter Lily and Calla lilies, or Arum lilies as they are called in some countries.

Fig. 29. Another whimsical setting features the Easter Bunny. This time, he appears on a white pitcher, holding a graceful crescent-shaped design of pussy willow, rose and pink alstroemeria, pink mini-carnations, and yellow mini-carnations with rose picotee edges. The pink lattice-rimmed plate is used with a decorated "Easter egg" salad/dessert plate. The yellow flowers repeat the yellow on the salad plate. The "cracked egg" salad bowl also adds a touch of piquant appeal. Pale pink napkin and soft green goblets are chosen as complementary components. (Deen Day Smith).

Fig. 30. A magnificent bronze angel, created by artist Clydetta Fulmer, holds an arrangement of yellow daffodils, yellow apples, small yellow asters, and various foliages. The delicate, scalloped edged china plate by Herend has a bright yellow and gold rim. Gold-rimmed, cut-glass stemware completes this elegant setting in which all components are exactly right for each other and in keeping with the religious holiday. (Deen Day Smith).

Mother's Day

Mother's Day is a fairly recent holiday in the United States. The first Mother's Day proclamation was issued by the Governor of West Virginia in 1910, and Oklahoma had celebrations that year as well. It was established as a national observance by Congress in 1911, the result of the extensive efforts by Anna Jarvis of Philadelphia. In 1914, President Woodrow Wilson proclaimed the second Sunday in May as Mother's Day, and this date has been unchanged since then.

Mother's Day is the third largest church-attendance day, after Easter and Christmas. It is traditional for those whose mother is living to wear a red flower — usually a rose or carnation — and for those whose mother has died to wear a white flower. In some areas of the country, the custom is to wear a pink flower in honor of one's living mother.

A much older observance, Mothering Sunday, is celebrated in England on the fourth Sunday of Lent. At this time, all children and those adult-children who no longer live at home spend this day with their mothers, bringing gifts and flowers.

This is an old custom, beginning long before the Reformation. A day honoring one's mother was the only permitted break in the vigorous observance of Lent.

In the 18th and 19th centuries, servants working away from their homes were given a holiday so they might visit their mothers on Mothering Sunday — one of their few days off from work each year.

Since World War II, many parts of England now refer to Mothering Sunday as Mother's Day, due to the influence of American soldiers who were stationed in England during the war, even though one is celebrated in May and the other during Lent. Mother's Day in the United States is celebrated on the second Sunday in May.

Fig. 32. The same design and most of the same appointments are used in this table setting, which is staged as an Exhibition Table Setting, Type I, for a flower show. Goblets of a soft green color were used instead of the amber crystal one. (June Wood)

Fig. 31a. A lovely table setting with an old-fashioned air honors Mother on her day. The theme was set by the antique RS Prussia china plates. They are hand-painted with soft yellow and white roses, with backgrounds of misty green. A green place mat is woven of fine straw with a lacy edging. The golden amber napkin repeats the colors of the roses on the plates. An amber goblet of fine crystal is an excellent color choice to complement the china. A green cherub container holds a delicate, nostalgic floral design of yellow roses, alstroemerias, freesias, white mini-carnations, and small-leafed foliages. (June Wood).

Fig. 31b. The hand-painted design motif of the antique RS Prussia plates can be seen well in this close-up view.

Father's Day

The United States did not have an official observance day honoring the nation's fathers until 1966, when a bill creating the holiday was signed into law by President Lyndon Johnson. The campaign to institute such an observance was successfully led by Senator Margaret Chase Smith of Maine.

The first recorded celebration of Father's Day was in West Virginia in 1908. Mrs. John B. Dodd of Washington State began a promotion in 1909 to have an observance of the day. Mrs Dodd campaigned extensively, and finally the city of Spokane, Washington widely publicized the idea and urged other cities to do the same. The Mayor of Spokane and the Governor of Washington proclaimed an official observance to be held on June 19, 1910. In 1924, President Calvin Coolidge supported the idea, but no official action was taken until 1966, when Father's Day finally became a national holiday.

No other country, other than the United States, has such a day honoring its fathers. Father's Day is celebrated on the third Sunday in June each year.

Fig. 33a. A rustic theme is appropriate for this Father's Day setting. The salad plate featuring a Mallard duck was the inspiration for the table. A wooden service plate, smoky brown goblet and wooden candleholders with copper-colored candles are all distinctive and compatible appointments. Linens are a brown and beige tweed place mat and a spruce green napkin, held by a ceramic Mallard napkin ring. The arrangement of beige shaved cattails, dark brown pencil cattails, assorted dried grasses, curly kiwi vine and rust alstroemerias features a ceramic Mallard duck figure, placed on a brown-stained bamboo base. (June Wood)

Fig. 33b. The salad plate which was the inspiration for the setting seen in Fig. 33a is shown in close-up.

Fig. 34. Traditional colors of red, white and blue spark this patriotic setting for a Fourth of July party. Twin Uncle Sam candleholders hold red tapers aloft. They wave tiny flags, which are placed in front of the design, and not within it. A red plate holds a blue and white star-shaped salad/dessert plate. A red napkin and blue goblet complete the place setting. The decorative unit consists of a rhythmic piece of decorative wood, painted blue, and dried allium Christophii seedheads, which are painted red to simulate exciting "fireworks". The container is a white ceramic cylinder. (June Wood)

Fourth of July

Parades in large cities, small towns, villages and hamlets; picnics by families or entire towns; barbecues; patriotic pageants and impassioned speeches; huge fireworks displays and small children with "sparklers": all are part of our nation's exuberant birthday celebrations on the Fourth of July. All of these are popular ways of celebrating the American Independence Day. This most American of all the holidays commemorates the adoption of the Declaration of Independence on July 4, 1776 by the Continental Congress in Philadelphia. The Fourth of July did not actually become a legal holiday until 1941, but to most of us, it seems to have always been a part of our national heritage. It is now celebrated in all fifty states, the District of Columbia and territories of the United States. The Fourth of July observance means a great deal to all Americans. It is interesting to note that three of the early Presidents, instrumental in achieving our country's freedom, died on July 4. They were Thomas Jefferson, John Adams, and James Monroe.

The United States flag is a symbol of the love and respect we owe our country, so we must always be careful in how we use it. It is never placed *within* a floral design, but is always in front of or above the design. When it is flown at our home or business, it should never be allowed to touch the ground, and should not be flown after dark or in inclement weather.

Colors used for Fourth of July celebrations are those symbolic of the flag — red, white and blue. Uncle Sam and eagles are also much featured in July 4th observances. The caricature of Uncle Sam, recognized by all as one of the symbols of the United States, was a creation of the 19th century cartoonist, Thomas Nast, the man who also gave us our popular image of Santa Claus.

We also celebrate other patriotic holidays, such as Flag Day on June 14, George Washington's birthday, Abraham Lincoln's birthday, Columbus Day, Memorial Day on the last Monday in May, and Labor Day on the first Monday in September. The same color scheme of red, white and blue would be used for these holidays, as well as with other symbols of our country.

Halloween

Halloween is a holiday adapted from an English one, called All Hallows'Eve, which was probably adapted from a Druid celebration. In the United States, it is a secular festival, mainly for children. Originally the fun was in playing "tricks" on friends and neighbors unless a payment of "treats" had been made to avoid the practical joke "tricks". Halloween is an occasion for dressing up in costume and going from house to house asking for treats. This October 31st holiday is symbolized by black cats (the companions of witches), pumpkins, witches on broomsticks, owls, skeletons, and the colors of orange and black.

The Legend of Jack-O'-Lantern

Irish immigrants brought the custom of Jack-O'-Lanterns to America. According to legend, Jack was a terrible, dastardly drunkard. One day he tricked the Devil into climbing an apple tree to pick its fruit, and while the Devil was in the tree, Jack cut the sign of the Cross into the tree's trunk. The Devil was afraid to climb down past that powerful symbol. Fearing reprisals, Jack made the Devil promise not to seek revenge on him for this trick by trying to take his soul. After Jack died, he was turned away from the gates of Heaven because he had been such a mean and drunken man. Seeking a final resting place after having been rejected in Heaven, Jack went to Hell, but was also turned away from there by the Devil. The Devil did help a bit by giving Jack a burning coal from Hell to light his way. Jack was eating a turnip at the time, so he put the coal in the turnip to make a lantern. Since then, Jack has constantly traveled the earth with his Jack-O'-Lantern in search of a place to rest. In Ireland, children carved out turnips and potatoes to light the night on Halloween. When the Irish immigrants came to America, they brought this custom with them, but found that a pumpkin made an even better lantern. It is said that's how the custom of lighted, carved pumpkins came into being on Halloween.

Fig. 35. A round piece of dried wisteria vine, painted black, frames this clever Exhibition Table Setting, Type II, to be exhibited in a flower show. Another black-painted root, like a jagged lightning bolt, breaks the space on that side of the design, creating interesting enclosed spaces at the same time. Appointments are a shiny, square black plate and a black contemporary goblet. An orange and black printed napkin is tied like a necktie for a creative touch. Two black wrought-iron cats, wearing orange bowties, are an added note which the children will love. An orange Bird of Paradise flower supplies variety of form and adds a balancing area of color. (Deen Day Smith).

Fig. 36. A table setting for an adult Halloween party is whimsical, yet sophisticated. We know it's Halloween because the smiling pumpkin face of the salad/dessert plate tells us so! It is placed on a square black dinner plate, with a pebbly-textured, shiny black plastic place mat underneath. The rolled black napkin is held by an orange pumpkin napkin ring. Black wrought-iron candlesticks, orange candles, and a black goblet complete the setting. The decorative unit is composed of dried palm fronds, painted black, with aspidistra leaves and orange pincushion proteas arranged on a shiny black plastic scrolled base. A lead cupholder, painted black, serves as a container on the base. (June Wood).

Thanksgiving

Thanksgiving is the United States' oldest holiday, a special national celebration of gratitude. It was first celebrated in early Colonial times in New England by the Pilgrims. The actual origin was probably inspired by the harvest festivals that the settlers would have remembered from their earlier life in England.

Harvest festivals were not restricted to those English celebrations, however. In Biblical times the Hebrews held one called the Feast of the Tabernacle; ancient Greeks held harvest festivals in honor of Demeter, the goddess of the harvest; and the Romans celebrated Cerealia in honor of Ceres, the goddess of grain.

The Pilgrims had lived through a very difficult period by the time their first harvest was finally safely gathered in. They had arrived in the New World in mid-December of 1620, so they could not plant any crops. As Governor William Bradford sadly said, "they had now no friends to wellcome them, nor inns to entertaine or refresh their weatherbeaten bodys, no houses or much less townes to repaire to, to seeke for succoure". They began building their first communal house on Christmas Day, a house, as Governor Bradford said, "for commone use to receive them and their goods". It was only twenty feet square, and it burned a few weeks later in a time of bitter cold. During the next nine months, they built seven houses, which were very inadequate shelter from the harsh weather for so many people. Supplies they had brought with them were almost exhausted, so many died that winter. When spring finally arrived, only fifty-five of the original one hundred and two original settlers were still alive.

Seeds they had brought with them from England had not germinated or grown well in their new home. Neighboring Indians, the Wampanoags (also known as the Pokanoket), came to their rescue by giving them seeds of corn and squash, then teaching them how to grow these crops which were new to them. The Indians also taught the Pilgrims how to hunt and fish in the woods and streams of this strange new land which was so unfamiliar to them.

After the first harvest in the New World was completed by the Plymouth colonists in 1621, Governor William Bradford proclaimed a time of thanksgiving and prayer, which was shared by all of the colonists and neighboring Indians for a period of three days. One of the colonists, Edward Winslow, wrote this account: "Our harvest being gotten in, our Governor sent four men fowling, so that we might after a special manner rejoice together after we had gathered the fruit of our labor. The four in one day killed as much fowl, as with a little help beside, served the company almost a week. At which time, amongst other recreations, we exercised our arms, many of the Indians coming among us, and among the rest their greatest King Massasoit, with some ninety men, whom for three days we entertained and feasted, and they went out and killed four deer, which they brought to the plantation and bestowed on our governor, and upon the captain and others."

Gradually the custom developed in New England of annually celebrating a day of thanksgiving after the harvest. By the 18th century, a Thanksgiving holiday was celebrated in Connecticut, Massachusetts and New Hampshire by proclamations of the states' governors.

During the American Revolution, a yearly day of national thanksgiving was suggested by the Continental Congress. Most celebrations during this time seem to have been related to successes by the Continental Army on the battlefield. There was a national day of thanksgiving on December 18, 1777 after the defeat of General Burgoyne at Saratoga. After the British surrender at Yorktown by General Cornwallis in October, 1781, Congress proclaimed a period of thanksgiving.

President George Washington proclaimed the first official national Thanksgiving Day on November 26, 1789, during his first year in office. In the following years, only Presidents John Adams and James Madison followed his example in proclaiming national Thanksgiving Days. Other presidents left the decision to state governors because there was an acrimonious debate going on, fostered by the clergy, who declared that the civil government had no right to proclaim a national religious holiday.

In 1817, New York State adopted Thanksgiving Day as an annual custom and by the late 1840s, Thanksgiving was being celebrated in Connecticut, Massachusetts, Vermont, Maine, Rhode Island, New Hampshire, Michigan, New York, Iowa, Illinois, Missouri, Indiana, Wisconsin and Pennsylvania.

In 1846, Sarah Josepha Hale, the editor of *Godey's Lady's Book*, began a diligent effort to have the last Thursday in November established as a national Thanksgiving Day. Mrs. Hale's magazine was very influential at the time. Each November she devoted the November issue of the magazine to the promotion of this idea. She wrote articles and editorials urging the declaration of the holiday, and also informing her readers exactly how the holiday should be celebrated. During the Civil War, she wrote letters to all of the governors requesting their help in having a national holiday proclaimed.

In 1863, President Abraham Lincoln declared a day of thanksgiving to celebrate the Union Army's victory at Vicksburg. His proclamation read: "I do set apart Thursday, the 6th day of August next to be observed as a day of national thanksgiving, praise and prayer to render homage due to the Divine Majesty for the wonderful things He has done in the nation's behalf, and to subdue the anger which has produced and so long sustained a needless and cruel rebellion, and finally to lead the whole nation through the paths of repentance and submission to the Divine Will back to the perfect enjoyment of union and fraternal peace".

Mrs. Hale was still not satisfied, however, because she wanted a national holiday which would be on a fixed date and celebrated each year, rather than one which was celebrated only to commemorate certain other events as they occurred. Finally, at her urging, on October 3, 1863, President Lincoln signed a proclamation naming the last Thursday of November of each year to be a fixed and annual date for a nationwide Thanksgiving Day. He stated that it was to be "A day of thanksgiving and praise to our beneficent Father who dwelleth in the heavens".

Since then every President has issued a Thanksgiving Day proclamation, designating the fourth Thursday of November as a national holiday. The only change to this was during the Depression, when President Franklin Roosevelt changed the date of the holiday. In order to encourage more spending and to aid in the nation's economic recovery from the Depression, in 1939 President Roosevelt moved the Thanksgiving celebration up a week, prolonging the Christmas shopping period. In the past, the day after Thanksgiving was regarded by most people as being the beginning of the Christmas season. (Unfortunately most stores are now displaying Christmas decorations before Halloween. Hopefully this practice will not be moved up to Labor Day or the Fourth of July!).

On May 20, 1941, President Roosevelt returned Thanksgiving to its original date, the fourth Thursday of November. On December 26, 1941, with Public Law #379, Congress fixed this date as the permanent official date for the national holiday of Thanksgiving.

Harvest and thanksgiving festivals are an inheritance from the times when agriculture provided the primary livelihood for most people. England celebrates harvest festivals, with parish churches being decorated with flowers, fruits and vegetables. Corn dollies are made to decorate the hay and corn ricks. Harvest suppers are a part of the celebrations. Canada has celebrated Thanksgiving on the second Monday in October since that date was officially set in 1957.

In the United States, Thanksgiving is a traditional family feast-day, where roast turkey and other traditional foods are the order of the day. Turkeys are native to the United States, and have long been associated with Thanksgiving Day dinner.

Since the holiday occurs in the autumn, traditional colors are beige, brown, gold, orange and rust. Symbols are turkeys, cornucopias, wheat, fruits and nuts, with an overall feeling of abundance.

If football is a part of your family's Thanksgiving Day activities, that too is traditionally-based. According to legend, at the original feast the colonists and Indians played stool ball, which was a cross between football and a type of croquet, and then they had other contests such as foot-races.

Fig. 37a. A Thanksgiving table setting was inspired by the lovely turkey figurines. They are a featured part of the decorative unit, which includes flowing-lined bare branches, dyed a coral-brown color; apples; feathers; bronze foliage and yellow chrysanthemums on a walnut burl base. The china plate has a motif of apples, nuts, wheat and feathers around its rim. A wooden service plate is used underneath the china one to provide contrast in color and texture. A coral linen tablecloth, rust napkin with a carved wood napkin ring, and a brown crystal goblet complete the setting. (June Wood).

Fig. 37b. Shows the plate which is so suggestive of Thanksgiving, in a close-up view.

Fig. 38. An Exhibition Table Setting, Type I, for exhibition in a flower show evokes the spirit of Thanksgiving. The exhibit is creatively staged with two yellow frames. Components are a brown wooden plate, two smaller Majolica plates with a leaf motif and additional color-touches of red, yellow and blue. A golden yellow pressed glass goblet holds a napkin in the same shade. Two wood candleholders, with red candles, add balance to the design. A green tablecloth and another yellow napkin are draped over the top of the frame to create a pleasingly proportioned space. A turkey basket holds red carnations, dried grasses and colored foliages. This is a delightfully colorful and beautifully coordinated Thanksgiving setting. (Deen Day Smith).

Christmas

Christmas has many different meanings to each of us. It is a special family-time, and Christmas is also our most treasured and widely celebrated Christian holiday. Christmas in the Christian Church is an annual festival held on December 25 to celebrate the Nativity (or birth) of Jesus Christ. Christmas celebrations have been noted by Christians since the fourth century

St. Nicholas of the fourth century, a Christian prelate and patron saint of Russia, is traditionally associated with Christmas celebrations. Legend tells of his giving surreptitious gifts to the three daughters of a poor man, who was unable to provide them with dowries. From this event supposedly has grown the custom of gift-giving on the Eve of St. Nicholas. Christians also associate the giving of presents with the gifts brought to the Christ Child by the Magi.

Santa Claus, that jolly, bearded little man, dresses in a red suit trimmed with white fur, flies through the sky in a sleigh pulled by reindeer, and slides down chimneys on Christmas Eve to bring gifts to good children. He is an American creation, inspired by the 19th century drawings of the newspaper cartoonist, Thomas Nast. Santa Claus is probably an adaptation of the Dutch San Nicholas. In England, he is called Father Christmas and in Russia, Father Frost. Whatever he is called, he is such a wonderful part of our Christmas celebrations, bringing joy to children. Other aspects of the celebration also incorporate such adapted customs as the use of holly and ivy, mistletoe, Yule logs and Wassail bowls.

Legend says holly berries were once white, but that Christ's crown of thorns was made of holly, so the berries became red from his blood and remained red thereafter. Another legend has it that robins were originally all-brown birds, until one tried to aid Christ on the cross. Its breast became smeared with His blood, and thereafter all robins have had red breasts. Early Christians hung holly boughs on their doors as a symbol of their Christianity. Holly and other evergreens were first chosen because they appear never to change or to die, so they had special religious symbolism.

The Christmas tree, an evergreen trimmed with lights and ornaments, is derived from the "Paradise tree", symbolizing Eden, which appears in early German mystery plays .The custom of a decorated Christmas tree probably first began in Strasbourg, France in the early 17th century. From there it spread to Germany and then to northern Europe. Prince Albert, husband of Queen Victoria, is credited with introducing the Christmas tree to Great Britain, and from there and from Germany, the custom was brought to the United States by immigrants from those two countries.The first recorded mention of a Christmas tree in America was that of Matthew Zahm of Lancaster, Pennsylvania in 1821. In 1830, in York, Pennsylvania, tickets were sold for six and one quarter cents for viewing a decorated tree.

The Crèche is a universal symbol of Christmas. St. Francis of Assisi is said to have created the first one, using the figures and the crib as described in the Bible. Christians feature it in their homes to commemorate the birth of Jesus Christ.

In England, Wales and parts of Canada, Boxing Day is celebrated on December 26. On this day, gifts of "Christmas boxes" are given to family and friends. It is a legal bank holiday in those countries. Advent is also celebrated in preparation for

Christmas. It begins on the fourth Sunday before Christmas, and is symbolized by an Advent wreath. One of its candles is lit each Sunday until Christmas. Children enjoy opening the little windows on Advent calendars, one for each day building up to Christmas.

There are many other now-traditional aspects to our Christmas celebrations. The poem, " 'Twas the Night Before Christmas", by Clement Moore is read to many children at Christmas. Mr. Moore wrote the poem in 1822 for his own children, and it was first published in the Troy, New York SENTINEL in 1823. This poem gives us many of our popular images of Christmas, such as reindeer, the sleigh, Santa coming down the chimney, etc. Carols and other traditional songs, such as "Rudolph, the Red-Nosed Reindeer" and Irving Berlin's "White Christmas" are heard throughout the land.

Fig. 39. Traditional colors of red and green are used in this table setting for an informal meal. A dark green service plate and a dinner plate of heavy red pottery with a Christmas tree motif are placed on a red runner, which has similar woven trees along its borders. A coffee pot, creamer and sugar on a tree-shaped trivet and a mug complete the appointments. A spruce green napkin is held by a tin Christmas tree, which opens to reveal a whirling figure for the delight of children. Red carnations, green and variegated hollies, and red nandina berries are arranged in a vegetable bowl from the pottery dinnerware service. (June Wood)

Fig. 40. A brass drum holds a decorative unit of " Harry Lauder's Walking Stick" branches (contorted filbert, or Corylus), red carnations, spruce branches and ferns. It and the appointments, consisting of a red plate, green service plate, red and green plaid-bordered salad/dessert plate and a brass goblet are placed on a dark green tablecloth. A red and green plaid napkin is held by a Santa Claus napkin ring. A spiraling brass candlestick holding a red candle adds needed height and interest to this festive holiday setting. (Deen Day Smith).

Fig. 41. Christmas china with a border motif of red ribbon and holly sets the theme for this lovely holiday setting. The plate is backed by a dark green service plate for additional color interest. A red goblet and a striking reindeer figurine add balance to the overall exhibit. A tall brass candlestick holds aloft a design of palms, red carnations and hollies. Another brass candlestick and red candle add needed visual weight to the right side of the design. (Deen Day Smith).

Fig. 42. The beautiful bronze angel (also seen in an Easter table setting in Fig. 30) holds a graceful design of holly, red carnations and feathery cedar branches. The elegant holiday setting is completed by a green marbleized service plate, an intricately patterned red and green Christmas china plate, and a dark green pressed glass goblet. A green napkin is held by an interesting brass napkin ring. All chosen components are beautifully suited to each other, and combine into a very lovely table setting. (Deen Day Smith).

Fig. 43. Lenox holly-patterned china, a cut-glass, gold-rimmed goblet and a brass angel candle-holder are elegant components for a holiday dinner. The tablecloth is textured metallic gold and two napkins are used, one is red with a pattern of gold and the other is ivory, which repeats the base color of the china. A tall red candle provides color interest. Holly, lacy needled evergreens, red carnations, nandina berries and gold glass ornaments are arranged in a low Mass design. The setting is festive even though all chosen components are formal in character. (Deen Day Smith).

Hanukkah

Hanukkah is an annual Jewish festival, which comes in December in most years. It begins on the twenty-fifth day of Kislev in the third month of the Jewish calendar, corresponding approximately to December in the Gregorian calendar. Hanukkah is also known as the Festival of Lights, the Feast of Dedication, and the Feast of the Maccabees. The holiday lasts for eight days, with a celebration being held each evening of those eight days.

Hanukkah commemorates the rededication of the Temple of Jerusalem by Judas Maccabee in 165 BCE, after the Temple had been profaned by Antiochus IV Epiphanes, the King of Syria and Overlord of Palestine. In 168 BCE, Antiochus had dedicated the Temple to the worship of Zeus, a pagan god, and had set up an altar to Zeus on the Temple's High Altar. Judas Maccabee led a Jewish army which defeated a much larger army, and recaptured Jerusalem in 165 BCE. He rededicated the Temple to God and put up a new altar to replace the profaned one.

According to one Talmudic tradition, only one small vial of pure olive oil which had been sealed by the high priest could be found for use in the rededication ceremony, but that small amount of oil burned miraculously for eight days. To commemorate this miracle, Jewish families have prayers on the first night of Hanukkah and light one candle. On the second night, two candles are lit, on the third night, three candles, and so on until on the eighth night eight candles are burning. These candles are held by a special candelabrum called a menorah.

Gold coins are often used on the table, or chocolates wrapped in gold foil. Gifts are exchanged and children play a game with a special spinning top, called a dreidel. Blue and white are the colors which are representative of the Hanukkah season.

Fig. HA-1. The colors of the flag of Israel, blue and white, are used in the decorative unit of this table setting, which commemorates the Jewish holiday of Hanukkah. A menorah with eight candles, a dreidel (which is a four sided top), and gold coins are traditional components which were used to interpret this holiday. (Deen Day Smith).

Birthdays, Weddings and Anniversaries

Birthday table settings can be especially fun and festive since they honor a special and specific person. It is important to consider the likes and dislikes, hobbies and any other particular interests of this person, and then to base the table setting on those rather than on your own interests or preferences. Signs of the zodiac, with the birthday celebrant's sign being used as a theme, is another possibility. The color of that month's birthstone could also provide a unifying theme. Birthdays are important to everyone, since they are one of the things which make each of us unique. Creating out-of-the-ordinary table settings for the "birthday boy" or "birthday girl" tells that person once again that we care and have gone to a little extra trouble to express this.

Weddings are joyous occasions. The degree of formality of the table setting will be determined by the time of day of the service and by the number of invited guests. A simple morning service limited to family and the closest friends would certainly not call for nearly as elaborate a setting as would an evening service with several hundred invited guests. Usually the colors chosen for the bridesmaids' dresses are also the colors used in table settings. Unless a seated meal is planned, most wedding tables will be set as buffet or reception tables.

Anniversaries too are usually very sentimental occasions. They may range in scope from a romantic dinner for two to a large party or reception for many friends and relatives. Any entertaining for anniversaries to celebrate the early years of married life for young people may certainly be casual and informal if you wish, but the major anniversaries, the 25th, 50th, or those commemorating even longer periods of married life, should be made as special and glamorous an event as possible. Traditionally, the color harmony for a 25th anniversary is based on silver, while the 50th is gold, and the 60th diamonds. These colors lend themselves to very lavish table settings.

Other special occasions meriting extra efforts in table settings might be baby showers and christenings, baptisms, Bar Mitzvahs, bon voyage parties and those for graduations, etc. Table settings for special family occasions are the ones which really should be given extra care and thought, since our families are the most important people in the world to all of us.

Fig. 44. An exuberant and adventurous table setting which would please a pre-teen or teenager on his or her birthday. The unusual and exciting color harmony is as bright and bold as contemporary music. A brilliant fuchsia tablecloth provides an unexpected contrast to the red and yellow napkins, the red goblet and shiny red container. Colors of plant materials: dried okra pods painted red, red carnations, small yellow asters, and bright yellow and hot pink chrysanthemums are all found in the brightly colored blocks on the plate, which provided the design inspiration for the table setting. (Deen Day Smith).

Fig. 45. "Mexican Fiesta: Alfresco Patio Party". Components used in this table setting have an earthy textural quality, giving the overall setting harmony and unity. The golden yellow soup bowl and under-plate with a corn motif are placed on a square wooden service plate. A gold place mat of heavy woven straw holds the dinnerware and Mexican glass goblet, which has an amber rim. A dark spruce green napkin with a wooden napkin ring repeats the green found on the corn plate. An arrangement of fasciated asparagus, bronze anemone-form chrysanthemums, unhusked corn, peppers, zucchini and large ivy leaves is displayed on a wooden service plate, which has been used as a base. The plant material is arranged in a heavy lead cupholder, painted brown and placed on the base. (June Wood).

PART THREE:

Table Settings For The Home

CHAPTER 5.
THE THEME'S THE THING.

By basing them on a theme, table settings can be lifted from out of the ordinary and the "every-day", to become something very special. Perhaps the chosen theme will be based on typical colors of a certain country, or on appointments and accessories made in a particular country. This type of setting would be especially appropriate for anyone preparing to leave on a long-planned and anticipated trip to a certain place, or for those returning from the featured country. Perhaps a local festival or celebration, or an ethnically-inspired celebration of a family member's or guest's personal background could be the inspiration for an exciting table setting. Thought given to selection of appointments and to the presentation of the carefully chosen menu can make these parties or family meals memorable.

It is hoped that attention to detail in the selection of components as well as setting the table carefully and correctly will result in lovely settings which will give much pleasure to your family and guests. This will provide a grace-note to our daily lives, not just at holiday time or when giving a party, but every day. The following are fresh and attractive examples of such table settings.

Fig. 46. "Portuguese Wake-Up Call: A Brunch With a Difference". What could be more cheerful for a delightfully appealing brunch setting than casual components chosen within a primary color harmony (red, yellow and blue)? The yellow pottery dishes, red and blue napkins, and gaily painted Portuguese folk art roosters are dramatically displayed on a black linen tablecloth. Red tulips, yellow lilies and black painted, swirling dried vines are arranged in a black wrought-iron antique teapot stand. This brunch setting has a special character all its own. (June Wood).

Fig. 47. "Vive-la-France: A Relaxing Meal By the Fire". Surely Coq au vin or Chicken Cordon Bleu would taste even better when served from this casual, but distinctive, table setting. The earthenware dishes have a coral and rust lattice-edging, with a center motif of coral gladioli, purple plums and eggplant, artichokes, mushrooms and bread sticks arranged in a basket. The dishes are complemented by a peach stemmed goblet, mauve napkin with a copper napkin ring, and a small pottery pot labeled "herbs of Provence". Peach and lilac gladioli, purple eggplant and artichokes, which are the same materials as those pictured on the plate, are arranged in a lovely copper jug. An over-turned copper augratin pan is used as a base for the decorative unit, repeating the color and texture of the container. A small purple cabbage and mushrooms are arranged at the base of the jug for balance and color-repetition. (June Wood)

Fig. 48. "Oktoberfest: Celebration of Autumn". The smoky, hazy colors of autumn are chosen for this smart table setting. A pewter flagon and a blue and gray salt-glazed crock from Germany are the keynotes, setting the tone for the table. A gray and blue handmade pottery plate and pewter goblet are set on a woven place mat of blue, with stripes in shades of honey-brown. A blue denim napkin with a carved wood napkin ring provide pleasing textural interest. The decorative unit of gray-blue bare branches, blue eucalyptus and agapanthus, white carnations, and an almost black foliage evokes a feeling of autumn's woods. The decorative unit is given more height and importance by its elevation on a wooden latticed trivet, which is of the same shade of brown as the place mat's stripes. (June Wood).

Fig. 49. "Chinese Elegance: A Dinner For Special People". The starting point for planning this glamorous table setting was provided by the very elegant pair of Chinese figurines. Their colors are repeated in the other chosen appointments: Thai celadon plate, soup bowl and porcelain spoon; glass goblet with brass stem; a golden place mat to echo the gold on the figures; and a peach linen napkin. Another celadon soup bowl was used as the container for the decorative unit. It is elevated on a carved wooden stand to give it added importance. Curled dried vines, painted gold, are used as line material in the arrangement, along with peachy-orange carnations and glossy dark green foliage. (June Wood).

Fig. 50. "Land Of The Rising Sun: A Unique Luncheon". The delicately lovely Cybis porcelain Geisha was the inspiration for this exotic table setting. It is featured in the decorative unit of curly dried line material, painted gold, and peach Gerbera daisies. A lead cupholder, painted dark brown to make it less obtrusive, holds the plant materials on an exquisitely carved wood Japanese table-stand. A rust-colored porcelain service plate, octagonal salad plate with a rust peony design, hammered brass goblet, and rust linen napkin are placed on a golden fan-shaped place mat. A knotted gold napkin ring and wooden chopsticks complete the setting. (June Wood).

Fig. 51. The same setting as shown in Fig. 50 is photographed against a deep blue background. Note how the colors have been changed and intensified by this simple change in background color. (June Wood).

Fig. 52. "Hawaiian Luau: Festive Patio Party". A bold and dramatic decorative unit would lend itself well to placement on a buffet table. Vertical lines of natural bamboo, black coral, orange and blue seafans combine beautifully with coral anthuriums and variegated ginger foliage. All are arranged on a bamboo scroll-ended base. Painted wooden tropical fish and a starfish complete a design with a strongly tropical flavor. A shell-shaped black plate and black glass goblet are placed on a heavily textured yellow place mat. Matching yellow napkin and a shiny black napkin ring complete the setting. For display purposes, one individual place setting is shown. On a buffet table, plates would be stacked, and other components grouped together in the most convenient and attractive manner. (June Wood).

Fig. 53. The same setting as in Fig. 52, photographed against a deep blue background. It illustrates how perception of color can be changed by placement, by adjacent colors, and by lighting. (June Wood).

Fig. 54a. The brilliantly colored and patterned plate, with its motif of deep blue grapes and red and coral apples on a bright yellow background, provides the starting point for this striking table setting. Another golden yellow pottery plate is used underneath it, and both are placed on a pleated navy blue place mat, along with a rust napkin. An octagonal peach glass goblet is in keeping with the other components. Peach gladioli, orange carnations, green grapes, Bird of Paradise (strelitzia) foliages and cut papaya are arranged in an antique scale, which has been painted navy blue. The peach colored flesh and large blue-black seeds of the cut papaya provide a luscious color note. The plant materials are arranged in a small bowl, which has been placed in the pan of the scale. The papaya would drip and discolor unless covered, so it has been covered with tightly stretched plastic film. The fruit is impaled on wooden skewers, which supply stems that can be forced onto the needlepoint. Take care that the skewers do not come through the flesh of the fruit. They should not be seen and should not be allowed to damage the fruit's appearance.

Of course, you may do whatever you like in your own home, and cut fruits and/or vegetables do provide a creative touch to decorative units, but you are only *permitted to do this in a flower show if the schedule states that is allowed.* If the use of cut fruits/vegetables is to be permitted in designs, it really should only be allowed in shows of short duration — those of one or two days at most — because the fruits and/or vegetables will begin to deteriorate, and will become very unattractive. Very soft-fleshed fruits and vegetables should also be avoided, since they will last for a much shorter time than will those having a firmer texture. It would be a very good idea for the schedule writers to include a short paragraph explaining this in the schedule, and including a list of those fruits and vegetables which last longest. It should also be stressed in the schedule that all cut fruits and/or vegetables must be tightly covered or sealed in some way. Cut fruits and vegetables should have the cut surface treated with lemon juice, liquid vitamin C solution, or one of the commercial products available for preventing unattractive darkening of fruits or vegetables, and the cut material should then be tightly covered with clear plastic film to prevent its attracting insects. (June Wood).

Fig. 54b. This picture provides a better perspective of the design of the plate used in Fig. 54a.

Fig. 55a. A sophisticated table setting with a contemporary feeling. Red anthuriums and aspidistra leaves are arranged in a black cupholder on a two-level black lacquered base. Sleek, silvery Nambé candlesticks with black candles are in keeping with the chic spirit of the setting. The motif on the china plate is one of red anthuriums with a gray stripe. The tablecloth and napkin are gray with a satin-weave gray stripe. (June Wood).

Fig. 55b shows details of the plate in Fig. 55a.

Fig. 56a. This is a fresh and crisp table setting for summer dining. Lemon-shaped pottery salad plates are placed on green leaf-edged plates. A lemon tureen and dark green napkins with bright yellow napkin rings are in keeping with the theme and colors used. Clear glass tumblers with bright yellow bases are a pleasing choice with other components. Sansevieria foliage, white chrysanthemums, yellow lilies, lemons and lemon foliage are arranged in a white latticed urn. In addition to its looking so bright and appealing, diners enjoy a wonderful fragrance from the lemons which have been used in the decorative unit. They are impaled on strong wooden skewers, which are thrust into the Oasis. (June Wood).

Fig. 56b shows the green leaf-edged plates used in the setting of 56a exceptionally well.

Fig. 57. Emphasis on color characterizes this lovely setting for a luncheon. A tall, graceful decorative unit of rhythmic willow branches, rose-red gladioli and blue-green eucalyptus sets the mood for the table. The botanical plates feature different herbs, but both are within the chosen color harmony and set the style for the setting. The flower motif on the container holding the decorative unit is very similar in feeling to the designs on the plates. Deep blue-green glasses echo the color of the eucalyptus. The rose-red napkins are an exact color match with the gladioli. This table setting achieves an exceptional degree of unity through skillful use of repetition and a wonderful sense of color. (Deen Day Smith).

Fig. 58. An unexpected but highly effective and original combination of colors gives unique élan and personality to this table setting. How many times have you ever seen these colors used together? Hot pink azaleas, yellow chrysanthemums, and golden daffodils are arranged in a brilliant yellow contemporary container. These same colors are seen in the botanical china plates, the napkins, and glass goblets. The lovely china is traditional in feeling, but the brilliantly colored rims on the plates, combined with the bright yellow in the decorative unit, gives it a whole new personality. This setting shouts, "It's spring!". It is delightfully fresh and vibrant in character. (Deen Day Smith).

Fig. 59. This table setting features exquisite appointments and a skilled blending of colors and textures. Flowers seen on the "Flora Danica" china are of the same character as the decorative unit which is composed of lilies, carnations, daisies, asters, chrysanthemums and ferns. Delicate cut-glass crystal is in keeping with the china, as is the cut-work, embroidered tablecloth. Linen napkins are used, as well as gold "Flora Danica" flatware. *Use of flatware is expected, of course, in table settings for the home. It is not permitted in flower shows, however, for reasons of security. This is true for both types of flower shows, Standard Flower Shows and Standard Home Flower Shows.)* (Deen Day Smith).

Fig. 60. A table setting with a very feminine aura, which is established by use of color and texture. Pink-rimmed china matches the tureen, which is used as a container for the decorative unit of pink tulips, "Stargazer" lilies and ferns. Cloth and napkins are of white linen. All appointments are beautifully compatible in spirit and in degree of formality. (Deen Day Smith).

There are a number of different types of table settings, based on the type of service. An *ALFRESCO* table setting is one which is set for dining outdoors. It may be a very casual occasion, either set on a table, on a cloth spread on the ground or even from a station wagon's tailgate. It might also be quite elegantly set on a lovely table on a terrace or sheltered patio. The quality of the chosen appointments and the occasion, as well as the setting, would determine the degree of formality of the table setting. Give special attention when planning a decorative unit for an outdoor occasion. It should be constructed in such a way that it cannot be blown over by the wind. For the same reasons, candles would not be used except those which could be shielded — by a hurricane shade, for example.

Benjamin Franklin was an innovative man, who has been credited with a number of inventions, one of which was supposedly the *BUFFET* service of meals. While Ambassador to France, Mr. Franklin wanted to invite a greater number of people than could be seated in his home for a Fourth of July celebration. He had food placed on a long table and his guests served themselves, then ate the meal while standing throughout Mr. Franklin's home and garden. He gave this party its name, a buffet supper. Webster defines *buffet* as being "a piece of furniture with drawers and cupboards for dishes, table linens, silver, etc." *or* "A counter or table where refreshments are served". Presumably, this is what suggested to Benjamin Franklin that name for a meal which would be served from such a piece of furniture. This kind of service for meals became quite in vogue among fashionable Parisians after that, and it is even more popular with hostesses and hosts of today.

For entertaining in today's homes, people often choose this style of entertaining because of its ease of service, since few of our present-day households enjoy the luxury of servants. This type of service might be used for breakfasts, brunches, luncheons, or dinners. It is necessary that the setting of the table be carefully planned so that everything is placed in a logical manner, allowing guests to serve themselves without any need to go backward and forward, or having to hold too many objects at the same time while trying to serve their plates. Service will usually proceed in this manner: the guests pick up their plates; then serve themselves with their choices of foods; then pick up napkins, silverware and beverages last. Placing components on the table in this manner will allow guests to have their hands free to serve themselves comfortably and with ease. Care and thought must also be given when planning the menu, so that the food which is to be served can be easily eaten with only a fork if guests are to eat while standing or from plates on their laps. If guests are to be seated at tables after having served their plates, this will not be a problem.

TRAYS have become almost as important to our current lifestyles as dining tables. Many of our meals are eaten from them. They offer portability and convenience for eating by the television, for luxurious breakfasts in bed or for serving someone who is ill. The trays themselves should be stable and not easily overturned. If they are to be carried, everything on the tray must also be chosen and placed in such a way that the essential stability is assured. This requirement for stability also includes any flower arrangement which is to be placed on the tray. Think of a tray as being a "table-on-the-move" or a "table-in-transit". Most meals eaten from trays are informal ones, and more casual appointments would be usually be suitable for them, but for such occasions as breakfast in bed for Mother on Mother's Day, for a birthday or anniversary treat, or for some other special occasion, more elegant appointments would be chosen.

Families may have tea in late afternoon, and the service is usually fairly informal, even if fine appointments are used. Tea parties, however, are usually more formal and elegant affairs. They are often thought of as being primarily feminine occasions, but this is not necessarily true.

In a number of cultures, the service of tea is an important one, and has numerous customs attached to it which must be observed. The Chinese feel that tea should only be drunk from fine porcelain. The Japanese have conceived an elaborate ceremony for the service and drinking of tea. The contemplation of lovely utensils and the enjoyment of the tea's aroma are considered to be as important as is the appreciation of it's flavor. The English, of course, have made observance of tea time an important ritual of daily life.

The drinking of tea has an interesting history. The Chinese Emperor Shen Nung was known as the Divine Healer because he was so interested in the use of medicinal herbs. On an herb gathering expedition, he noticed that the drinking water he was boiling had a very pleasant aroma and a refreshing taste. He then noticed that some leaves from the wood he was using as firewood had fallen into the pot of water. These leaves were from a nearby Camellia sinensis plant. The tea plant, while a member of the same family as Camellia Japonica, the flowering shrub of gardens, has many botanical differences when the two are compared.

Tea was first used in China as a medicinal herb, believed to be helpful in repairing damage to eyesight, as well as for relief of fatigue. As time passed, tea became important in the culture, with a number of rituals important to its preparation and to the drinking of it.

The Japanese took some of the Chinese rituals, adapted them, and made from them their own national observances for tea ceremonies. In Japan, flower arranging and designing of gardens came to be seen as related to the tea ceremony, even thought they are all separate art forms. In fact, *chabana*, the special flower arrangements used for tea ceremonies, are very different from the traditional Japanese art of flower arrangement, *Ikebana*.

In *chabana*, the flowers are meant to be admired for their own beauty, and not for the skill or method of their arrangement. Only seasonal flowers are used, and they are placed casually in their container so they look as if they are growing naturally, without having been "arranged". They are placed very simply in the container in their natural state, without any artifice. Flowers picked from the garden or in the mountains or fields are used; those bought from florists which have been cultivated or grown under artificial conditions, such as in greenhouses, are strictly forbidden by tea masters. The container which is used is an object intended to be examined and admired. The fragrance of incense is also incorporated into the ceremony, one which is intended to gratify all of the senses.

The East India Company was developed for the exporting and distribution of tea, and it became the most far-reaching, most powerful trading organization the world has ever known. Tea was first imported into Holland in 1610, into France in 1636, and into England in 1650. Tea was a prized commodity and was very expensive, so only the most affluent among the upper classes were able to enjoy it. The English even developed special boxes, called a caddy, for storing tea. As greater amounts were imported, the drinking of tea spread to the middle classes, and finally to the lower classes as well. The first tea shop was opened in London in 1884, and soon one could be found in almost every city block. Originally all tea was imported from China, but tea from India began to appear on the market in the 19th century, and today India is the world's largest exporter of tea.

We owe the modern custom of serving dainty morsels of food with tea to the wife of the Seventh Duke of Bedford, who lived in the early 19th century. This idea was embellished and developed by the English into what is now called "high tea". Tea was brought to America in the late 17th century, and soon became our most popular drink, as it was in Mother England. Tea time became the most popular form of entertaining.

Tea tables are usually set with fine linens, delicate china and lovely floral arrangements, usually arranged in a traditional manner.

There are, of course, many other types of tables: Reception tables; formal and semi-formal dinner and luncheon tables; tables for all sorts of special holidays and occasions, as well as tables with themes; picnic and barbecue tables; and tables for everyday family dining. There is an infinite variety of kinds and types of tables, which is one reason the designing and setting of them is so very interesting.

Fig. 61a. Very elegant and delicate components with a feminine quality were chosen for this lovely tea table. The beautiful china has a motif of swags of pink roses, with touches of gold. The formally balanced, traditional flower arrangement contains flowers which are compatible in color and texture to the china: pink and rose carnations, pink lilies with a deep rose throat, and ferns are arranged in a footed compote of fine china. Delicate cut-work and embroidered linens are also used, with their colors repeating those of the other appointments. Crystal and brass candlesticks provide balance to the overall design. (Deen Day Smith).

Fig. 61b shows all of the exquisite details of the china used on the lovely setting seen in Fig. 61a.

PART FOUR:

Table Settings For The Flower Show

CHAPTER 6.
IN THE WINNER'S CIRCLE!
AWARD-WINNING TABLE SETTINGS

Winning a coveted blue ribbon in a flower show is very exciting, and winning a Top Award is even more exhilarating! To be a consistent winner takes a great deal of work and study, as well as a lot of planning and preparation. You will never be a consistent winner if you have become convinced that you already know everything and have nothing further to learn, merely because you have won several times in the past. Neither will that exhibitor be a winner who has become lazy and complacent after having won several awards, resorting to the repetition of the same ideas and excessive reusage of the same components which won in the past. Real winners are those exhibitors who are forever working to refine and expand their knowledge and skills.

Having the right attitude toward exhibiting will make this hobby fun, as it should be, and will determine your success to a large extent. You should approach every flower show and your participation in it with the attitude that you will make every effort to win. This does not mean that you do this because you feel you must win a blue ribbon for every entry you make, and neither does it mean that you will be the type of exhibitor who pouts if you do not win, telling everyone who will listen that, "The judges obviously did not know what they were doing. Anyone with eyes to see can tell that *my* exhibit is the best!". It simply means that you will strive to make all entries as perfect as you can make them, for the sake of your own pride and for the viewing public's enjoyment and education.

The Flower Show Schedule

Once it has been written, printed and distributed, the schedule becomes "the law of the show". All exhibitors, and certainly all judges, should read the entire schedule carefully before preparing entries for competition and before starting to judge in a show.

Those serving as Chairman of the Schedule Committee or members of the committee should be among a club's most experienced members. Their task is to prepare a schedule that is as accurate as possible in the use of correct terminology and in following guidelines established by the *National Council of State Garden Clubs, Inc.* A good schedule must include all general information needed by exhibitors, such as times and date when entries will be accepted; where entries are to be made; hours the show will be open; time of judging; when entries must be removed; and general rules for entries. The Schedule Committee will also choose an appropriate theme for the season and for the place where the show will be staged; consider abilities of the expected exhibitors, especially for exhibitors in the Design Division; take into account the availability of seasonal plant materials which should be expected to be in prime condition at the time of the show; keep in mind the availability of staging properties, or have a realistic idea of what properties the club can afford to make or acquire; plan for a proper balance between Horticulture and Design Divisions; use correct flower show terminology, as specified in the HANDBOOK FOR FLOWER SHOWS; plan for interesting, attractive and innovative staging of designs; keep in mind the available space for the show; work within a budget; and see to it that all information needed by exhibitors and judges is included in the schedule.

Once you, the exhibitor, have decided to enter a flower show, a thorough reading of the schedule is your first step. Having read the schedule, you will then decide which classes appeal to you, and which ones you would like to enter. If the chosen class requires you to make an advance reservation, the next step would be to call the person who is accepting reservations and tell that person you would like to enter a specific class. Once having made a reservation to enter, you are obligated to make an entry in that class in the show, or else to find a substitute to make that entry if you are unable to do so yourself.

Before beginning the work of planning what kind of exhibit you will do and of assembling your components, reread the schedule so that you are *positive* about what the schedule is telling you to do in the particular class you will enter, in other words, what kind of table setting is wanted in the class (luncheon, dinner, tray, tea, buffet, etc)?

- Is the table to be Functional or Exhibition?

- What is the theme, or the occasion? The schedule should state this.

- What is the expected degree of formality? If it is not spelled out in the class description, then the title will be the indicator of what is wanted.

- How many place settings are required, if the schedule is allowed by the HAND-BOOK to specify this in the particular class?

- What constitutes a place setting, if the schedule states this?

- Are you required to use a specific type of plant material in the decorative unit (i.e., all fresh; all dried; or designer's choice)?

- What are the size limitations for staging? The schedule must be very specific about type, size and method of staging, unless exhibitors are allowed to provide their own creative staging within an allotted space.

- Where and how will the exhibit be staged?

If your exhibit is to meet all schedule requirements and avoid losing points because of failure to conform, then you must be very sure that you understand all schedule requirements, and you must keep those requirements in mind while preparing your table setting for the flower show. No matter how creative and unique your concept, or how lovely your components might be, or how skilled your craftsmanship and your execution of the overall design, if you did not follow the schedule it is very unlikely that the judges will reward you with that coveted ribbon.

If the class you have chosen to enter is one eligible to receive the Creativity Award, the schedule *may not* specify what kind of plant materials will be used in the decorative unit, the only exceptions being those entries in a class requiring a Botanical design (an unlikely requirement in a class of table settings) or if it is a plant society's show. In those shows, designers may be required to use the particular type of plant material featured in the show in all designs. In all other shows, the designer is free to use all fresh materials, all dried, or a combination of the two, as well as having the freedom to use other components in the arrangement if they wish. The schedule may specify type of staging to be used.

Special Rules and Flower Show Policies

These are found in the HANDBOOK FOR FLOWER SHOWS. On those pages explaining the Special Rules and Flower Show Policies, exhibitors are told of certain rules and policies which will *always* apply in flower shows. (These have been paraphrased by the author, but the meaning and requirements are the same as expressed in the HANDBOOK.):

(1) All exhibits must contain some plant materials, whether fresh and/or dried, as specified in the schedule. Plant materials are classified as foliage, blooms, fruits, vegetables, etc.

(2) No artificial flowers, fruits, vegetables, or foliage are ever permitted. The exhibitor, Classification Committee and judges should use common sense in this regard, however. A vegetable tureen in the shape and color of an eggplant or squash, for example, should not be considered to be artificial plant material and should not be disqualified or penalized for that reason. It is a functional piece which had its inspiration from nature, and it is not trying to masquerade as a *real* eggplant or squash. Many lovely and exciting serving pieces, containers, napkin rings, etc., are being made in the forms of various fruits, vegetables, flowers and leaves, and these do not fall within the realm of being considered to be artificial plant materials. It is those which are made of some man-made materials, *attempting to imitate real plant materials and used as such* in designs which we do not ever permit in flower shows.

(3) Only one exhibit is permitted by an exhibitor in each class or subclass.

(4) Each design entry must have been created and placed by only one exhibitor. There may be special separate classes or sections in a flower show, with classes

specifically written for participation by clubs. In these classes, clubs would be competing against other clubs, not clubs against individuals.

(5) Plant materials need not have been grown by the exhibitor unless required by the schedule. Exhibitors are permitted to buy plant materials or to use those obtained from the gardens of others unless the schedule says otherwise.

(6) Fresh plant materials may not be treated in any manner, which includes artificial coloring. The only exception is that a slight amount of embellishment of fresh foliage may be permitted by the schedule in a holiday show. Glycerinized plant material is permitted only when specified by the schedule. This rule which prohibits artificial coloring or treating of fresh plant materials applies to those bought from florists, as well. When told that those turquoise or emerald green carnations, for example, are not permitted in designs brought for entry in a flower show, occasionally an exhibitor may be heard to protest, "But I bought it this way from the florist!". This is never an excuse, and there is never an exception to this rule, other than that for holiday shows which is described above and in the HANDBOOK.

(7) Dried and/or treated plant material is permitted only when this is stated in the schedule. (The exceptions being in those classes eligible for the Award of Distinction, where it is *required* that all plant materials used in the designs must be dried, and in those classes eligible for the Creativity Award, where the designer has complete freedom of choice of plant materials and components, with one exception: rules state that artificial plant material is never permitted. The schedule may also be written in such a way that exhibitors are given this same freedom of choice in other classes and/or sections, with the exception of those eligible for the Tricolor Award or Award of Distinction.)

(8) Contrived flowers and/or plant forms must be made of recognizable plant materials (fresh and/or dried), and are permitted only when specified by the schedule.

(9) Cut fruits or vegetables, or prepared foods are not allowed *unless permitted by the schedule.* Cut foods must be sealed in some manner to discourage insects. Many exhibitors, and even some judges, are under the impression that cut fruits or vegetables can *never* be used. This is not true. If the show's schedule is written in a way which allows this to be done, the exhibitors may choose to use cut fruits and vegetables in designs.

Other important rules and requirements which will be found on these same pages of the HANDBOOK are:

• The use of flatware is not permitted in a tables section or class. The schedule could permit the use of inexpensive ware such as wooden chopsticks, plastic ware, etc. if desired. The intent of this policy is to protect expensive flatware from loss or theft. There would not be the same concern for those other mentioned things, so the schedule might permit their use if the schedule's writers wished to give exhibitors this additional freedom of choice.

· Such things as birds' nests, stuffed birds (real birds, not crafted ones), butterflies or other insects, or fish are not used in designs in flower shows. *National Council of State Garden Clubs, Inc.* is a conservation-minded organization, and as such, does not wish to aid the destruction of wildlife by encouraging their use in flower shows. For the same reason, no feathers may be used other than those naturally shed ones from such domesticated birds as chickens, turkeys, peacocks, etc. The schedule must specify that the use of feathers is permitted. The use of such things as coral, seafans, sponges, bones, antlers is permitted. The designer is expected to exercise good taste in their use.

· Proper respect must be shown to the United States flag. It is never used *within* a design, but is always shown above or in front of a design.

· A Madonna should not be used on the table during a meal. Proper respect should be shown for the Madonna, as well as to other religious symbols, such as the Star of David, St. Francis, a crucifix, etc.

· Living plants with exposed roots may be used in designs. The designer is not required to sever a plant from its roots in order to use it in a design. This allows the designer to use rooted plants, which can then be repotted after use so they can continue growing. It also means vegetables with roots, such as scallions, and other plants with their roots visible may be used in designs if those roots are clean and free of dirt. It is very possible that such plants with visible roots will add a note of beauty and distinction to the design, if chosen and used with taste and discretion. Moss may be used if desired. However, plants growing in containers are not allowed to be used in designs.

· Accessories or features may be used, unless prohibited by the schedule.

Functional Table Settings

A Functional Table is one which is set as it would be for the actual service of food. It will include dishes, crystal (or other types of glassware or drinking utensils of metals, plastics, etc.), linens and floral design, or designs if multiple arrangements are used, but not valuable flatware for reasons of security. Accessories and features may be used unless prohibited by the schedule. Features may not be used in classes or sections eligible for the Tricolor Award or Award of Distinction, however, because the HANDBOOK requires that there be an emphasis on plant material in all designs eligible for these awards.

When evaluating a table setting as a whole, there must be an impression of order and convenience — the feeling that you could actually sit down at the table and eat comfortably from it — as well as that essential impression of harmony and unity. All of the components used on the table should be in keeping with each other. They should be within the same range of quality and degree of formality, and should be compatible with each other in color, texture and scale. Those chosen components must then be arranged on the table in such a way that the proportions created by choice, arrangement, and placement are pleasing ones.

The schedule will provide specific rules and descriptions of what is expected from the exhibitors in all sections and classes of table settings, abiding by those rules and requirements within the HANDBOOK FOR FLOWER SHOWS. For Functional tables, the schedule may or may not specify the number or make-up of place settings, depending on the schedule's requirements.

There may be classes of Functional table settings for any of the following types of settings in a flower show:

- *Alfresco*: A table for outdoor dining. Literally translated, alfresco means "in the cool". Service may be casual, informal or semi-formal, depending on the type of meal and quality of appointments. The schedule will be your guideline to what is expected.

- *Buffet*: A table which provides for the service of food, but it is one at which no one is seated. Buffet service is considered to be informal, regardless of the type or quality of appointments because diners serve themselves from it. The chosen appointments may be of the finest quality, or they may be of the most casual, such as plastic or paper. Tablecloths may be floor-length if desired. When evaluating a buffet setting, ease and convenience of service, as well as the beauty of the overall design are important points to evaluate. When judging buffet tables in a flower show, the judges may not pick up the appointments since they are never allowed to touch an exhibit, but they should *mentally* "pick them up" in order to determine if appointments are placed logically and functionally so that guests could serve themselves easily and comfortably, without the difficulty of having to hold too many components.

  The schedule will be the indicator of what would be acceptable for use in the flower show, since the title or class description will tell the exhibitor the occasion for the setting, thus indicating the expected degree of formality. Four or more settings are expected on a buffet table setting in a flower show.

- *Reception:* Similar to a buffet table since guests serve themselves from it. May be either semi-formal or informal. Arrangement of components may be symmetrical (semi-formal) or asymmetrical (informal). In either case, the tablecloth may be floor-length if desired. The occasion will determine the formality of chosen components. Ease of service is very important. In a show, there should be service for at least four on a reception table.

- *Semi-formal:* Closely related to a formal table setting, with the major difference being that professional servers are needed for formal tables/occasions. Classes are never written for formal tables in shows sponsored by *National Council of State Garden Clubs, Inc.* On both semi-formal and formal tables, the decorative unit is placed in the center of the table, there are even numbers of place settings and all components are arranged symmetrically. Appointments of high quality would be chosen. Tablecloths are usually white, ivory, ecru or pastels, with napkins matching the cloth. Fine quality place mats, such as those of lace, cut-work or embroidery, and others of fine textured materials are also acceptable.

- *Informal:* A much more casual mode of dining. There may be even or uneven numbers, with asymmetrical placement of decorative unit and of other components if desired. Chosen appointments are of less formal textures and colors.

· *Trays:* Components should be well-proportioned to a limited space, and all should be in scale with each other. Avoid having the overall setting look cluttered, so only essential items should be included. Remember, all must be stable, including the decorative unit, since the tray has to be carried. Close attention should be paid to compatibility of color and texture, so that the overall effect is one of harmony. This is very important for tray settings since the total area is small, and all components will be in very close proximity to each other, inviting comparisons.

The two following table settings are Functional settings. Anyone could sit down and eat comfortably at these tables, with all needed components in place with the exception of flatware, which is not used on flower show table settings.

Fig. 62. A Functional table setting, using the same tablecloth seen in Fig. 63. This setting has a completely different style from the one in Fig. 63. In this setting, the feeling is traditional, with an interesting interplay of ideas due to the selection of a fine china, which has a scalloped edge of pale orange, and delicate crystal. A traditional Mass design of orange carnations, apples, alstroemeria, ferns and leucothoe foliage is arranged in a fine china compote, which matches the dinnerware. The peach colored linen napkin has a lace edge, repeating the shape of the china's rim. (Deen Day Smith).

Fig. 63. Another Functional setting which incorporates components with a striking contemporary feeling, all combined into an inviting setting. The textured linen cloth has a woven striped pattern, and it sets the color harmony for the table setting. Black plates, goblets and napkins provide bold contrast, while the orange pottery salad plates match the orange found in the cloth. A creative decorative unit features orange pincushion proteas, cedar, and a curved dried vine painted black, all arranged in a heavy pottery container. (Deen Day Smith).

Exhibition Table Settings: Types I and II

Exhibition Table Settings are seen only in flower shows or in displays. They have nothing to do with the actual service of food, and are intended solely as design exercises using creative concepts. Their primary purpose is to show the artistic coordination of the varied components which have been used, and they usually utilize creative staging. These table settings are never groupings of unrelated objects, but always must convey an impression of dining. The schedule *may not* specify what items are to be used, such as the number of place settings or what pieces make up a place setting, but it must state how much space exhibitors will be allowed in order to stage their exhibits. There may be classes of Exhibition Table Settings for the following types of tables: alfresco, buffet, informal, reception, semi-formal, tea, trays, etc., just as there may be classes for these same types of tables in classes of Functional Table Settings.

Within the broad overall category of flower show table settings called Exhibition Tables, there are two types: an Exhibition Table Setting, Type I, which includes components used for dining and completed flower arrangement(s), or decorative unit(s), and an Exhibition Table Setting, Type II, in which there is *no* completed floral design (decorative unit). Plant material must be present in these Type II tables, but it is used simply to supply needed color, texture, form, or balance due to its placement in the overall design. The purpose of this type of setting is to show the correlation of plant materials to other components, i.e. *what* plant materials would be best to use with the chosen components, but not *how* to use them in an arrangement. To put it in its simplest, most concise terms, the only difference between these two types of Exhibition Table Settings, Type I and Type II, is in the way in which plant materials are used - whether there is a completed decorative unit included or not.

The class title will indicate to the exhibitor what the occasion for the setting would be, or the class description may specifically state the occasion or theme. In any case, the schedule must leave the exhibitor in no doubt about what type of table setting is to be created. The exhibitor should then decide what degree of formality and what type of appointments would be suitable for the given title or occasion. The schedule must, however, allow the exhibitor *complete freedom* to choose the kind and number of components to be used in creating Exhibition Table Settings, as well as their placement within the design. That old idea which some judges still express, that some sort of serving piece must be present in order to indicate what is to be served, is incorrect. This is not what the HANDBOOK says about choice and use of components in an Exhibition Table Setting, either for Type I or Type II. The schedule may not (and therefore, *judges* may not) make any requirements about what the makeup of table appointments must be in these classes.

For example, an exhibitor might choose one dinner plate from a patterned service, a solid-colored salad plate, two stemmed goblets, and three napkins. The plates might be stood on edge, hung on the background, or suspended within the staging device, or staged in any manner the exhibitor wished. The two goblets might be needed for balance, and could be placed in any manner the exhibitor chose — one might be turned upside down with the second one on top of it, base-to-base, or one might be upright and the second over-turned, lying on its side, etc. — in other words, components may be placed in any way the exhibitor chooses in order to aid the appearance of the overall design. More than one napkin may be used for special color effect if desired. These might be folded together, they might be hung someplace in the design, they might be placed in cups, mugs or glassware, etc. — however the designer wishes, and the possibilities are endless. Remember, in Exhibition Tables, the items used are chosen for their contributions of color, form and texture, with no consideration given to functionalism, but there still must be that essential impression of being for *dining* if the exhibit is to be classified as a table setting.

Fig. 64. An Exhibition Table Setting, Type I, in which components are staged in a non-functional manner, but no special staging props are used. Three plates, of differing designs but with related colors, are all staged in upright positions. For balance in the overall design, the brass goblets are placed on the left side of the decorative unit instead of to the right of the plates, as they would be on a Functional table. Strelitzia leaves, white carnations and orange pincushion proteas are used. This exotic setting would be suitable for New Year or for many other occasions. The schedule controls use of painted dried materials, as well as embellishment of foliages in a holiday show. (June Wood).

Fig. 65. Another Exhibition Table Setting, Type I, this time a frame within a frame is used, with both being incorporated into the design. Because of the distinctive components used — a black and white star-shaped salad/dessert plate with a gold edge, black china service plate, brass goblet, and black and gold napkins with a star napkin ring — this glamorous setting, too, would be suitable for a New Year's party setting or for any other occasion. A creative touch is seen in the use of two stacked "Man-In-the-Moon" cups, which serve as a container to hold the design of black and gold painted line materials, white carnations and aspidistra leaves. A spiraling black and gold candlestick holds a black taper, adding needed height interest, and also filling its space well. (June Wood).

Fig. 66. A cheerful and earthly Exhibition Table Setting, Type I, has a sunflower theme. The theme was set by the tablecloth with big, bold sunflowers printed on a black background. Texturally compatible plates also provide interesting textural contrasts within the overall design. A wooden service plate is used with a shiny black pottery plate and a golden-orange salad/dessert plate with a sunflower motif. The pottery container also has a raised sunflower design, and it holds an arrangement of dried sunflowers with fresh aspidistra leaves. Two stacked green goblets fill their space attractively, as do the three napkins of black, brown and golden-yellow, which add pleasing repetition of colors. (June Wood).

Fig. 67. A bold and dramatic Exhibition Table Setting, Type I, relies on striking forms and an exciting use of color to tell its story. Three different plates of varied shapes are used: a white one with zigzagging black lines is placed on a square black one in the upper corner, while a black shell-shaped plate is placed in the lower corner. Three black goblets are placed where needed for balance, with each of the three being placed in a different position – upright, upside down, and lying down. The bold, but open forms of the black painted dried palm fronds contrast beautifully in form and in color with the red carnations. The container is a shiny black circular one of interesting design. The blackamoor figurine adds interest as well as balance to the overall design. (Deen Day Smith).

Fig. 68. The two black frames are incorporated into this stunning design by hanging the black and red runner over the top of the larger frame and extending it over the smaller one. The interesting metal container provides exciting elements of space and texture. It coordinates well with the swirling black line materials and the red carnations. The bold red plate matches the two napkins, which are placed to provide excellent color balance and equation of interest. The parrot plate and mug introduce notes of dynamic color as well as variation in pattern. Placement of the two black goblets is exactly right for their space. The overall exhibit is beautifully proportioned. (Deen Day Smith).

Fig. 69. Color is the reason this exciting setting shouts, "Look at me!". A blue frame of interesting shape and enclosed spaces is incorporated into the overall design. A brilliant yellow runner with blue fringed edges delineates the space. The golden yellow service plate and napkin are exact matches to the runner, while the dinner and salad plates provide variations in pattern and color. A blue goblet is an excellent choice to introduce the secondary color. The tall, slender, orange wrought-iron container gives needed height to the overall design, and lends importance to the decorative unit of orange carnations, bittersweet vine, ferns and Chinese lanterns. (Deen Day Smith).

Fig. 70. Creative staging of two smaller frames within one large one gives a dynamic impetus to this Exhibition Table Setting, Type II, within a horizontal space. The two smaller frames are filled by two cork place mats, which become backgrounds for other components. A lighter colored wooden service plate and three inlaid-wood plates with mosaic designs introduce variations in texture and pattern. Two black goblets and a patterned cup and saucer give needed variations in height for added interest to the overall design. Chosen plant materials are a Japanese honeysuckle root and orange pincushion proteas. These choices in plant materials are well-suited in color, form and texture to the other components. (Deen Day Smith).

Fig. 71. An exciting use of color and pattern give this bold contemporary Exhibition Table Setting, Type I, special personality and drama. A black wooden container holds black painted line materials, yellow lilies, spotted aucuba and yellow candles. Another tall yellow candle in a simple black candlestick balances the overall design. Yellow napkins also aid balance due to their placements. The spiraling black metal napkin rings repeat the lines of the swirling dried vines in the decorative unit. The blackamoor figure also holds a yellow lily, supplying needed color balance. The black and white patterned plate creates a focal area for the overall design and provides some necessary contrast for interest. The lines in the plate also repeat the triangular lines of the container in the decorative unit. (June Wood).

Fig. 72. This Exhibition Table Setting, Type I, is a very cheerful setting suitable for a breakfast table. The Italian straw rooster crows "Good morning!" to one and all. A scalloped black plate provides an interesting form, contrasting with the round white plate with a pattern of black and white chickens. They are displayed on a shiny black plastic place mat, with a bright red napkin. Two mugs of varied sizes also hold bright red napkins, carrying the eye through from the bottom to the top of the design. The red circular container introduces space and airiness in the center of the overall design, a feeling which is reinforced by the openness of the black line materials. Red carnations and green aspidistra leaves add needed color and texture. (June Wood).

Fig. 73. The two Balinese dancers supply the exotic inspiration for this Exhibition Table Setting, Type I. The exhibit incorporates two turquoise horizontal frames. The unexpected color combination of coral, purple and turquoise is carried out by the purple service plate and turquoise soup plate; napkins; turquoise balloon-shaped goblet; coral lilies, purple and lavender gladioli, and the colors of the two figurines. Color coordination and placement are the keys to this setting's feeling of harmonious unity. (June Wood).

Fig. 74. An Exhibition Table Setting, Type I, employs no special staging, but components are staged in a pleasing grouping and in a non-functional manner. The brilliant orange pottery service plate and the blue and orange sun-face patterned plate are elevated, with the royal blue and bright orange napkins threaded through one orange napkin ring, and placed to create a continuously flowing visual line. Two royal blue Mexican glass goblets are placed so that they also continue the same flowing line direction as the napkins. The sun-face motif on the brass candlestick repeats the design of the plate. The tall orange container is partially hidden by the plates, assuring its visual incorporation into the overall design of the setting. Lilies in two shades of orange, variegated ginger foliage and sansevieria leaves complete the decorative unit in this setting with an exciting Mexican theme. (June Wood).

Fig. 75. This Exhibition Table Setting, Type I, has a Christmas theme. Two identical floral designs are placed on each side of a gold lacquered service plate and a holly patterned china plate. Cut-glass goblets are placed at the top and also to one side of the plates to provide balance. The table cloth is a gold metallic fabric. The two arrangements contain beautiful gold and white candles, gold glass ornaments, white carnations, spruce, cedar and variegated holly. These candles are the perfect example of why judges should not demand that candle wicks must be charred in a flower show setting. Decorative candles such as these are often used simply as the beautiful accessories that they are meant to be, and they are not meant to be burned. In an actual home situation, they would probably never be lit. There is no requirement in the HANDBOOK that there must be some indication that candles used on flower show tables will be burned — in fact, the opposite is true. The HANDBOOK states that wicks need *not* be charred. (Deen Day Smith).

Fig. 76. An Exhibition Table Setting, Type I, has a more informal mood, which is established through use of texture. A pottery Christmas angel holds red carnations, lotus pods, holly, cedar and red leucothoe foliages. The red and green plaid napkin is circled by a napkin ring made of the same plant materials as found in the decorative unit, which is a creative idea. The bright red plate is attractively backed by a wooden service plate. The heavy red pressed glass goblet and the green candleholder are of pleasingly compatible scale and texture. The dark spruce green cloth provides an excellent colored background for the other components. (Deen Day Smith).

Fig. 77. An Exhibition Table Setting, Type I, Christmas table has a very different feeling from the previous two settings (Figs. 75 and 76), even though they too are for the holidays. This lovely composition has a pastel color harmony and delicate components with an appealing feminine quality. Two porcelain angel figurines are the inspiration, and they are combined with pink-rimmed china, which has a centered motif of hanging Christmas ornaments. An iridescent pink goblet, gold metallic tablecloth, and lace-edged napkin are all in keeping with the other components. A tall, elegant decorative unit has airy sprays of wheat, some of them painted gold, and pink carnations to complete the beautiful setting. (Deen Day Smith).

Fig. 78. This and the following two Exhibition Table Settings, Type I, all have the same decorative unit, showing how components of the right coloring, textures, and character can be interchangeable. The arrangement is of dried coral bush shrub branches, which establish the linear structure of the design, combined with rust alstroemerias, dark red chrysanthemums, bronzed leucouthe foliage, and red and yellow "Gala" apples in a footed wooden compote. In this setting, a deep coral plate, orange/blue/green salad plate and a blue goblet are used. Deep coral, royal blue and dark red napkins provide color repetition and balance to the overall design due to their placement. (June Wood).

Fig. 79. The same decorative unit as in the previous Exhibition Table Setting, Type I, is used with different appointments. A delightful plate has a design of a stylized chicken, with head and tail of deep red and golden yellow. A wooden service plate provides contrast in color and texture. Napkins of deep rust and dark red repeat colors found in the plate. Two heavy amber glass goblets on the opposite side of the arrangement provide balance, and repeat the golden-yellow found on the plate. (June Wood).

Fig. 80. A third setting incorporates the same decorative unit as in the two preceeding pictures. This time, two deep red and golden yellow plates in the shape of apples are used, repeating the colors and the apple motif of the decorative unit. The amber glass goblets are pleasing color repetitions, as are the three napkins of rust, dark green and deep red. This would be a great setting for the celebration of Johnny Appleseed Day. (June Wood).

Fig. 81. Achromatic (neutral) colors of black and white, with an accent of bright red, combine in a bold and dynamic contemporary Exhibition Table Setting, Type I. A shiny black square container holds red anthuriums, airy foliage, and a very rhythmic piece of decorative wood, painted white. This gives the wood the effect of a bolt of lightening moving through the design. A piece of red fabric attached to the back of the frame provides a background for the decorative unit, as well as for the black square plate which is hung on it. Two zigzagging black wrought-iron candleholders repeat the lines of the wood and add additional rhythmic movement. A black goblet and patterned napkins are in pleasing proportion to the enclosed space in which they are placed. (Deen Day Smith).

Fig. 82. An Exhibition Table Setting, Type II, has a nautical theme. A fish net, dyed navy blue, is draped over the matching blue frames. A piece of orange tree root flows smoothly through the design. Orange lilies and deep red Japanese maple branches add color and balance, and show a pleasing relationship to other components, but they do not constitute a finished flower arrangement. These plant materials are chosen to show their correlation to the other components: orange fish plates and clear glass goblets with blue rims and bases. The deep blue candlestick with orange candle and orange napkin provide additional color interest as well as balance for the overall design. (Deen Day Smith).

Fig. 83. An Exhibition Table Setting, Type II, is staged within two red horizontal frames. A dark green pottery plate with swirling leaf edge combines with a pottery salad plate, which is hand-painted with a design of several different vegetables. A matching green pottery candlestick is partially hidden behind the plates, making it an integral part of this visually complete unit. A red candle completes this picture, also supplying needed height in the filling of its space. Filling other spaces, and equating interest and visual attraction throughout the overall design are a green cabbage tureen and under-plate; a green cabbage leaf sauce boat and under-plate; and a red pepper covered sauce tureen and under-plate. Two olive green glass goblets are stacked base-to-base on the top of the frame for added height and balance. Red and green napkins are chosen for color interest and repetition. Fresh red peppers and large ivy leaves provide the required plant material (*not* in a finished arrangement), as well as color and textural contrasts. (June Wood).

Fig. 84. Cool colors in varying shades of blue and green give a restful feeling to this Exhibition Table Setting, Type II. A rounded blue juice glass with green stem and base holds aloft a very tall and slender green wine glass which has a blue stem and base. They provide height and balance to the overall design. Three napkins in blending shades of deep blue-green, green, and blue flow downward beneath a blue-green glass cup and saucer. Two exquisite blue and green Venetian glass birds provide rhythmic forms and add a distinctive note to the composition. A compote was made by gluing a blue-green glass goblet and plate together. It is filled with polished glass cullets of a matching color. A large blue Venetian glass plate with blue and green textured bubbles backs a blue-green luncheon plate. Deep blue agapanthus flowers and large aralia leaves are placed where needed as color accents and for balance. (June Wood).

Creativity Through Staging:

While the schedule may not specify what components an exhibitor may (or *must*) use for Exhibition tables, it *may* specify the type of staging required, such as a background, niche, or frame of specified dimensions. The schedule may specify required components on Functional tables if the schedule writers desire, but may not specify what kinds of plant materials must be used, unless the exhibit is entered in a class or section eligible for the Tricolor Award or the Award of Distinction or in a plant society show. If staging "props" are to be furnished by the Show Committee, then the schedule must give the dimensions and color of them. The exhibitor may not paint or change the color of the furnished staging devices unless the schedule specifically gives permission to do so.

If exhibitors are allowed to furnish their own creative staging, then the schedule must inform each exhibitor of the dimensions of the space each will be allowed in which to stage the exhibit, and the completed table setting must stay within the allotted space. Allowing exhibitors this freedom of furnishing their own innovative staging will encourage more creativity, and will enhance the beauty of the show. If the schedule permits this option of staging the exhibit in a creative manner to be determined by the exhibitor, one or more frames, cubes, boxes etc. may be used if desired. Components can be placed on top of the staging device(s), within them, in front of or to the sides of them, or be suspended within them. Other staging devices could be utilized as well, such as crates, Plexiglas stands, other types of stands, tea carts, picnic baskets, etc. The exhibitor's imagination would be the only limitation.

Schedules should be very carefully worded if the intent is to allow exhibitors as much freedom as possible. Many of the problems in judging seem to arise because the schedule is incomplete, ambiguous, not worded precisely enough. Rules and requirements in a schedule should never be just lifted bodily from a previous show's schedule without first checking thoroughly to be sure that those rules comply with the current HANDBOOK, and that any changes appearing in THE NATIONAL GARDENER have also been followed in compiling the show's rules.

Without the necessary careful thought, the schedule's wording may impose limitations which its writers never intended. For example, if the schedule says, "using a frame", then components may be inside, hung on, or be outside the frame. If the schedule says, "within a frame", it means *exactly that* and all components must be within the inside boundaries of the frame. If the schedule states, "incorporating a frame", then some components must be outside the boundaries of the frame so that the frame becomes a definitely integrated part of the overall design. The schedule writers should be very clear in their own minds what they want the exhibitors to do, or what they are permitting them to do, and then should phrase the schedule so that the intent is clear to exhibitors and to judges.

The schedule must also state whether an underlay is permitted to extend over the front edge of the table on which an exhibit is staged, otherwise the exhibitor may be penalized if the underlay is allowed to extend beyond the stated allotted space. In a flower show, an underlay is that which is placed underneath a design, but it is *not* a base. It may be of matboard, fabric, or whatever material the exhibitor wishes. It is usually used as a visual continuation of the background in order to give a pleasing continuity for the design, but it may be of a contrasting color if desired. When an underlay is used as a part of a design or an Exhibition Table Setting, it is usually a piece of fabric or some other material on which the staging device(s) and the other components of the design are placed in order to unify the overall design. An underlay may also be used as an underskirt on a Functional Table Setting, with the table cloth placed on top of it. In this case, the underlay's purpose would be to hide unattractive table legs or parts of other staging.

The 1987 edition of the HANDBOOK was the first to allow exhibitors to create design exhibits which extended beyond the outside dimensions of staging devices, such as backgrounds, niches, frames, etc. Exhibitors should be aware, however, that they *do not* have unqualified permission to do this whenever they please. Designs are only permitted to exceed the staging device's outer dimensions *when and if* the schedule specifically permits them to do so. If a design extends beyond the allotted space without permission by the schedule to do so, then that design should be penalized under those points allotted to proportion in the Scale of Points which is used for evaluating that particular design. Points would also be lost for failure to conform to the schedule. Broadly speaking, a frame of reference is a visual boundary established by the objects surrounding a design. If a staging device such as a background, niche or frame is used, then the actual dimensions of these devices establish the frame of reference for that particular design. An exhibitor can only exceed those established boundaries if the schedule states that the staging device is to be incorporated, thus giving the exhibitor permission to allow parts of the design to go outside of the dimensions established by that particular staging device. In that case, the schedule should then state the dimensions of each exhibitor's alloted space.

Fig. 85. An Exhibition Table Setting, Type I, "*using* a frame", allows the exhibitor to go outside the frame, if desired, and to stage the components in any manner the designer chooses. In this case, the innovative staging consists of two hula hoops which are glued together for added stability and are then bolted to a wooden base. The whole staging device is painted black. The container for the decorative unit is a white wrought-iron rooster. It holds red carnations, bronze (almost black) foliages and curled dried grasses which are painted black. The curly form of the line material repeats the lines of the rooster's tail. Some parts of the decorative unit do extend outside the frame, which would be allowed by a schedule worded, "using a frame". An interesting salad/dessert plate provides the design inspiration for the table setting. The plate pictures two black and white chickens "behind chicken wire", their brilliant red combs adding additional color interest. The red plate which completes the place setting echoes this color. The tall white candlestick and red candle provide needed height, and break up the space on that side of the design. The black napkin, knotted around the candlestick, is a creative touch. A bold striped underlay ties the whole exhibit together visually. (Deen Day Smith).

Fig. 86. This Exhibition Table Setting, Type I, (with a decorative unit) is staged *within* a frame. You can see that this does not inhibit creativity, even though components are within the dimensions established by the frame. The perky gingham printed and flowered plates are hung on the back of the frame, backed by peach basket lids, painted pink. Another of the same kind of plates is elevated at the base for variety and interest. A lime green napkin and glass goblet repeat the frame's color. Wooden lathe strips painted pink are off-set to provide additional depth for the decorative unit of zebra grass and pink caladium leaves. (Deen Day Smith).

Fig. 87. An Exhibition Table Setting, Type I, *incorporates* a frame. A crisp black, white and red color scheme unites this exhibit. A black tablecloth fills one section of the uniquely designed frame. All components are in turn staged on a black and white striped underlay, which provides unity to the setting. The chosen components of red and white plates, individual white cabbage tureens, and a black mug are all compatible in texture, color, scale, and degree of formality. Placement of the red napkin is attractive and interesting. A very exciting and rhythmic Creative Vertical Line Design provides added drama to the setting. Red anthuriums, philodendron and aralia leaves, and flowing bare branches are arranged in a black wrought-iron container with two levels. (Deen Day Smith).

Fig. 88. This exciting Exhibition Table Setting, Type I, proves that a table setting staged with a background does not have to be dull or out-dated, but can be very creative. The background and underlay are of a rust fabric, a color which is seen in one of the feathers from the salad plate's design motif. A bright red runner and dark green napkin are draped over the top of the background, both with a pointed end for unity. The dramatic black plate and the unusual patterned plate and mug are highly compatible with each other and with the shiny black square container used for the decorative unit. Curled dried wisteria vines and contrived curled rattan forms repeat the brown tones from the dishes and the background fabric. Red gladioli and green hosta leaves repeat the colors of the runner and napkin. All combine into an exciting and harmonious whole. (Deen Day Smith).

Creativity and Distinction: What's the Difference?

The HANDBOOK FOR FLOWER SHOWS defines *creativity* as being an original concept in the choice of components or in the organization of the design elements within the limitations of the principles of design. Webster defines creativity as being inventive, imaginative, or being productive.

With the exception of a few unquestioned geniuses, such as Leonardo Da Vinci or Michelangelo, every one of us at one time was a beginner in the exercising of our creative abilities. None of us were expert flower arrangers at our first attempt. Some have more creative talents than others, whether due to our individual environmental differences, to genetic make-up or to differences in education, travels, or personal experiences — *why* is not important. What *is* important, is that each of us should make every effort to develop our creative skills to the fullest extent that we are able. Everyone can develop creativity!

There are many different approaches to developing creativity in our designs. One of the most important is to be willing to try new things and to be open to new ideas. Have an open mind, in other words! An inflexible mind means a sure death for creativity. Too many people approach a new style of flower arrangement in the same way in which some small children react to a new food or a new experience: "I *know* I'm not going to like it!". Before making such a judgment, why not study a new type of design thoroughly? Why not evaluate it according to how well the elements and principles of design were utilized, rather than being influenced by our personal prejudices and dislikes?

Always looking for new materials which might be incorporated into designs is another way to increase the creativity in designs. Examining materials at a hardware store, builders' supply, even the grocery store can often stretch our imagination. Many of these everyday things can be used creatively if you approach them in a new way. We often do not really *see* things in our everyday life: examine an article with a new intent — think of how you might change its color or texture, how you might combine it with some other thing you have seen or that you own. This is the essence of creativity: the development of a truly "seeing eye". Besides making our designs more creative, it has the added benefit of making our journey through life more exciting as we become truly aware of all that is around us. We've been given such a beautiful world, so why not enjoy it with all of our senses? As Jonathan Swift said, "May you *live* all the days of your life."

To be creative, it is not always necessary to find or buy *new* materials. Even more important to utilizing creativity in our designs is developing new ways of using materials or components which we already have. Perhaps you might combine one container with a second container (or more). You might turn a container, a piece of wood or some other component on its side or upside-down, rather than using it the same way you have always used it in the past. You might stack containers, or "stagger" them, placing one slightly in front of and to one side of the other. Really *look* at all the containers, accessories, bases, pieces of wood, dried materials, etc. that you own, then experiment with them, trying new ways of using them.

Introducing an usual combination of materials and components is another way of gaining creativity in designs. Look for new shapes, forms, colors, patterns, and then look for other components which would enhance these qualities through repetition, or boldly contrast with them. Inexpensive containers which you may find at flea markets or junk shops can be painted any color you like if their original color is not attractive, or if they are not the color you need for a particular design. In this way, components of designs can become beautifully coordinated.

Improve your skills and technique through *practice.* Having the most creative of minds, capable of constantly thinking of new and innovative ideas will be of no help to you if you can't make those ideas work! Every designer who hopes to do creative work must also become a skilled craftsman, with an extensive knowledge of mechanics. You must also develop the habit of giving your designs thorough and ruthless scrutiny, making needed changes and improvements as you work. Neatness and impeccability of detail are just as important to an outstanding design as is creativity, especially in designs which are intended for a dining table.

Adapting ideas from other arts and crafts is not plagiarism, and is nothing which we should be ashamed or reluctant to do. Voltaire said, "All arts are brothers", and he was correct in making that assessment. Adapting is not the same thing at all as copying. Adapting from other mediums means attending art shows, visiting museums, reading, studying, etc. to learn about new trends in the art world. Perhaps in studying a painting, sculpture, or some other art form, we will see a new combination of colors or textures which we had not thought of using before. These might be adapted to our own medium, which is plant material, and thus into a design. In doing this, we are following the correct procedure for all creative art work: first study, analyze, think; then accept or reject certain aspects of your design. All of it involves making selective and conscious choices, of arranging and rearranging, of ordering and reordering, which will result in your own personal creative concept for designs.

As surely as there are positive ways to aid and develop creativity, there are detriments to creativity. Copying the works of others is one certain way to hamper creativity since this is an approach which requires no special mental or creative effort from us. Far better than copying the works of someone else whom we admire is to create something of our own. Each of us can, and should, develop our own personal style of arranging, based on our own unique personality. Developing our own style, however, does not endorse allowing our arranging to fall into a never-changing way of doing things. When someone tells you, "I can always recognize your designs in a show", this was probably meant as a compliment, but it should ring an alarm bell for you that you need to develop some variety and to introduce more creativity into your work.

We must not be so timid and conservative in our approach to design that all originality and spontaneity is lost to us. A great part of that attitude is attributable to a fear of failure or of criticism. Many people are too anxious about what others may think of their work, or of being thought "different". Our culture must bear a certain measure of the guilt for insisting upon too much conformance in behavior and thought from each person as the price for being accepted. We must all have the courage to exercise our creativity, and to gain the personal satisfaction which comes from creating something that is truly our own. We must always consider all possibilities, both in our choices of components and in the way in which we combine them into an aesthetic whole. The great satisfaction which comes from creation is its own reward — winning a ribbon in a show is simply an *added* pleasure, and should never become an end within itself.

In addition to developing all of our creative instincts and abilities, we must develop the ability to evaluate our own designs honestly and unemotionally. No designer will ever improve in artistic development if he or she is unable to do this. Ask yourself a number of questions after a design is completed:

- Have I used anything in this design which would not be missed if it were removed?
- Is there too much emphasis in any one area of the design due to placement of a dominant form, or dominance of a color because of placement or amounts?
- Is there too much contrast of form, pattern, color or texture so that the overall impression is one of busyness or clutter?
- Is there too little contrast, so that the overall feeling is one of too much sameness, dullness, monotony?
- Is the design well-balanced, or is there an uncomfortable feeling that the whole thing may fall over at any minute?
- Are proportions of both the areas and amounts pleasing?
- Is the design rhythmic, with pleasing or exciting visual movement throughout, or is it static and uninteresting?
- Is the rhythm disturbed or interrupted due to careless placement of components?
- Is there an impression of depth, or does the design seem flat, with little incorporation of essential space?

By asking yourself these same questions which the show's judges will surely ask themselves about your design, you will be able to find any faults in advance and will be able to correct them. Then the judges' questions about your design can all be answered in a positive manner!

Distinction is an entirely different quality from creativity. The HANDBOOK FOR FLOWER SHOWS defines distinction as "marked superiority in all respects". It means the exhibit is as perfect as it is possible to make it. All components used must be in excellent condition, clean, and free from defects. Plant material must be fresh, crisp, well-conditioned and free from all evidence of dirt, insect damage or spray residue. The exhibitor's technique and craftsmanship must be so well developed that mechanics are not visible or distractive, and the whole exhibit should be neatly put together. Beyond that, however, an exhibit is not truly distinctive just because it is free from obvious faults, and is merely well-done and mildly pleasant in its appearance. Instead, it must have that superior concept and quality that sets it apart from all others, that makes viewers want to come back for a second look! The highly distinctive exhibit is one that has qualities marking it as truly outstanding, chic, dashing, charming, elegant, stunning, opulent, exquisite, exciting, avant garde, vibrant, dramatic, dynamic, or smart, etc. It is one that holds the attention of the viewer, and is superior without resorting to the bizarre. In actuality, it is possible for an exhibit to be very distinctive without being outstandingly creative, and it is also possible for an exhibit to be highly creative in concept, but to be so carelessly put together that it loses a great deal in distinction.

Judges should remember that any exhibit which has lost points in *design* qualities cannot be considered to be perfectly *distinctive*, so some points must be deducted from the total amount allotted to distinction in the Scale of Points used for that particular class or section. There is no set formula which tells you how many points to deduct, but the number of points deducted under design is in direct relationship to the degree of impairment to distinction, and will influence how severe the deduction must be under distinction.

Judging Table Settings

All judges' first step in preparing themselves to fairly evaluate the exhibits in a class or section of table settings should be to read and study the schedule thoroughly. Before beginning to evaluate any table setting exhibit, the judge should know what the schedule allowed or required the exhibitor to do in that particular class:

- What is the title?
- What kind of occasion, type of meal, theme does the particular title suggest? The schedule may specifically state these things.
- What degree of formality does the title suggest would be appropriate for the class?
- Does the schedule make certain *requirements* of the exhibitor: For example, does it specify how many place settings must be included in the table setting?
- Does it state what pieces will constitute a place setting?
- Does it require the exhibitor to use a certain type of plant materials in the decorative unit, either all fresh, all dried, or does it allow the exhibitor freedom of choice? (The HANDBOOK will govern this if a National Council Top Award is offered in a particular class or section.)
- Are accessories or features permitted or prohibited?
- Is the exhibitor permitted to use painted or treated dried materials?
- Are contrived forms allowed?
- Does the schedule allow exhibitors to cut fruits and/or vegetables for use in the decorative unit?
- How is the exhibit to be staged?
- Did the exhibitor follow all schedule restrictions and requirements?

Once the judges have answered all these questions to their satisfaction, they will then proceed to evaluate the merits of the exhibit itself. If the table setting is required to be a Functional setting, then these questions must be asked and answered:

• Does a sense of order and convenience prevail throughout the entire setting?

• Is the overall design harmonious and pleasing?

• Does the decorative unit obstruct the view of opposite diners? Is it too tall, too wide, too dense?

• Are components too crowded, making comfortable service of food difficult, as well as impairing the beauty of the table?

• Is the table too cluttered or too bare in appearance?

• Is the tablecloth of a length that might be caught and pulled by diners, causing an accident?

• Is the overhang too short, so the overall effect is one of skimpiness?

• Are components too near the table edge for safety?

• Are they uniformly set and spaced, enhancing distinction? All place settings used within a table setting must be identical in spacing and in placement.

• Are all components placed for easy, comfortable use?

• Are all components neat, clean, in perfect condition - in other words, free from chips, cracks, scarring, smudges, stains, dirt, etc.?

• Is the overhang even all the way around the table?

• Are linens clean, crisp, free from all wrinkles and unnecessary creases? Only one length-wise crease down the center of the table is permissible.

Judges should appraise the table first as a complete unit for overall perfection and relationships, and then they should evaluate individual details.

They will ask themselves whether the overall table is set in such a way that it is well balanced, due to the placement and distribution of components on it. Are the overall proportions of occupied space to unoccupied space pleasing? In other words, is it too cluttered or too sparse? They will evaluate the compatibility of colors of the chosen components, and the suitability of the choice of colors to the occasion and theme. They will do the same evaluation of choices and distribution of textures. They will ask themselves whether all components chosen are in correct scale to each other and to the table as a whole. They will certainly consider whether all components are compatible to each other and to the class title or theme.

Having done this for the table as a whole, they will then evaluate the decorative unit separately, and will ask themselves some of the same questions which were asked in evaluating the overall table setting:

• Is the color pleasing within the decorative unit itself, and also as it relates to the entire table?

• Is it in pleasing proportion to the table as a whole, and are the proportions within the decorative unit itself pleasing (i.e., the amount of plant materials used in relation to the container; the amount of one color in relation to amounts of other colors, the amount of one type of material in comparison to other materials used, etc.)?

• Is the design rhythmic, or is the rhythm static or interrupted?

• Are textures compatible within the design, and as it relates to the entire table setting?

• Is it in scale with the overall setting?

• Is it compatible in style, color, texture, degree of formality to other components, and is it suitable to the class title?

• Does it fit class requirements as to type of plant materials?

Judges are reminded that they should evaluate all tables classes which the schedule indicates are to be for a seated meal from a seated position. If the Show Committee has not provided chairs, the Show Chairman should be asked to do so if possible. If this is not possible, than each judge should study the table thoroughly while in a crouched position, so they are able to see the table as an actual, seated diner would see it. Don't worry about looking ridiculous to the clerks or to anyone else, your primary concern must be one of fairness to the exhibitors whose work you are evaluating. Buffet, tea and reception tables (in other words, those at which guests would be standing) are judged while standing.

If the tables to be judged are Exhibition Table Settings, these are judged according to how well the elements and principles of design were utilized, as any other design-type would be judged: whether there has been skilled use of color and texture; whether the overall design is well balanced, rhythmic; whether there is adequate employment of dominance and contrast to make the design interesting, avoiding monotony or dullness; whether there is too *much* dominance or contrast, so that other elements and principles are adversely affected; whether pattern has been utilized in such a way that there is enough variation for interest, but the overall design is not too busy; whether proportion and scale have been utilized skillfully and well. In evaluating these settings, there is no expectation that functionalism will be considered in any way. The exhibitor must have freedom of choice of components as well as for their placement in the overall design.

In evaluating table settings for flower shows, judges are urged against being excessively strict or too literal in the demands they make of exhibitors. While keeping in mind that the primary function of a flower show is to be educational, judges should guard against becoming so obsessed with minor technicalities or "rules" that they unduly penalize those entries of outstanding beauty, distinction and creativity. Of course, we need some rules and regulations for judging. These will assure a more standardized procedure for judging in all parts of the country, and a mutual vocabulary of terms will produce a much needed common ground for understanding and communication among judges. This in turn will provide for a more correct and fairer analysis of all exhibits. However, an obsession with "rules" (other than HANDBOOK requirements) to the point of inhibiting individual creativity and personal expression should be avoided. We should never feel it to be our responsibility as judges to impose total conformity in thought among exhibitors or an absolute uniformity in concept or execution of designs. What a dull world it would be if we were all alike! Always check the Scale of Points for judging a particular class, and avoid penalizing excessively for a relatively minor fault. This is not to say that standards should not be upheld, or that awards should be given to unworthy entries — the intent is simply to emphasize the idea that it is better to reward good qualities than to penalize for those faults which are really not all that important in the final analysis. Any criticism given by judges should always be constructive so the exhibitor benefits from it, and is never hurt by it.

Judges should approach any entry which they are to judge as free as possible from any preconceived idea of how the exhibitors should interpret a particular class title. The exhibitor might choose an entirely different approach to interpretation, use of color or texture, etc., and while this approach might be a different idea or concept from the judge's, it could be correct within itself and in fact, superior. One of our most revered presidents, Thomas Jefferson, said, "I tolerate with the utmost latitude the right of others to differ from me in opinion". Should we do less?

Exhibitors, in turn, need to cultivate certain attitudes for competing in flower shows. It is a good idea to remind ourselves occasionally that there are at least three others in competition in any particular class, and that each of them would like to win just as surely as we ourselves hope to win. The ability to empathize with others will help us develop that essential quality of good sportsmanship at flower shows. Exhibitors also need to develop a healthy perspective about competition. No one, no matter how talented, can expect to win with *every* entry made in *all* flower shows, so none of us should become angry, be too critical of judges and other exhibitors, or be too self-critical for not winning. Flower arranging and competition in flower shows, after all, should be a pleasant hobby and a means for stimulation to self-improvement in our particular art form, but it should never become the vehicle for excessive self-flagellation. A generous portion of humor and objectivity are definitely assets to be cultivated by the flower show exhibitor and competitor.

Scales of Points

In flower shows sponsored by the *National Council of State Garden Clubs, Inc.*, the Standard System of Judging and Awarding is used. This system allows only one blue ribbon (first place), one red ribbon (second place), one yellow ribbon (third place) to be awarded in each class or sub-class. One or more white ribbons (honorable mention) may be given, if merited.

Each blue ribbon winner must score 90 points or above; each red ribbon winner must score 85 points or above; each third place must score 80 or above; and honorable mention winners must score 75 points or above. Top Award winners must meet even higher standards — they must all score 95 points or more, and must meet all requirements set forth for them in the HANDBOOK FOR FLOWER SHOWS as well.

In this system, each entry within a class or section is judged against a standard of perfection (i.e., 100 total points), using a Scale of Points which has been compiled for judging all entries of a specific design-type or style. The schedule should indicate what Scale of Points in the HANDBOOK will be used for judging a particular section or class. These Scales of Points will assign each quality to be judged a certain number of points, which represent perfection for that particular quality. Total points for all these qualities will add up to a total of 100 points. For example, a Scale of Points to be used for table settings would assign points for the qualities of conformance to the schedule, for Design, for color and textural harmony, for distinction, as well as for creativity and expression.

If the table setting to be judged is required to be a Functional Table Setting, then points would be given for conformance, and under this quality, judges would be expected to evaluate the functionalism of each exhibit in the class; under Design, judges would evaluate the overall table setting, and then do the same for the decorative unit, so the total points for Design would be divided between these two separate evaluations. Design is always evaluated according to how well the exhibitor used each principle of design (balance, dominance, contrast, rhythm, proportion and scale). The elements of design would be considered, but only as they affect the principles of design. Color and textural harmony, distinction, creativity and expression, would also be evaluated. (Please consult the HAND-BOOK for a complete listing of Scales of Points.)

Winning a blue ribbon for your table setting exhibit in a flower show is wonderful, but winning a Top Award is the epitome of achievement! Competition for these awards is intense. To assure a certain level of competition, in order for any of these Top Awards in Design to be presented the schedule must be written in such a way that there is a minimum of three eligible classes for each of the awards; also there must be a minimum of four entries in each eligible class, for a total of at least twelve exhibitors in the competition for each award. If there are fewer entries than this, the award may not be given, no matter how high the caliber of the blue ribbon winners are in each of the three required classes. In any Standard Flower Show sponsored by the *National Council of State Garden Clubs, Inc.*, the following Top Awards are available:

• The *Tricolor Award* may be offered and presented to a blue ribbon winner, scoring 95 points or above, for a table setting in which *all fresh plant materials* were used in the decorative unit. The line material also must be of fresh plant material, and *may not* be such things as plastic, feathers, rope, metal, etc., even if the schedule allows accessories to be used. The HANDBOOK FOR FLOWER SHOWS is very specific in stating that the line materials in the design must be fresh plant materials. Decorative wood is not permitted in any form because decorative wood is considered to be dried plant material. Accessories may be used unless the schedule prohibits them.

Two Tricolor Awards may be given in a Standard Flower Show if all requirements are met. They might be given for two sections or groups of classes composed entirely of designs; two sections or groups of classes composed of table settings only; or one section or group of classes of designs and another section or group of classes of tables. It is also possible if only one Tricolor Award is given, that the make-up of the required three classes might be two classes of designs and one class of table settings, or vice versa, with a total of twelve entries or more. The Tricolor Award is represented by a rosette of red, blue and yellow ribbons.

• The *Award of Distinction* is offered and presented to a blue ribbon winning table setting, scoring 95 points or more, which uses *all dried plant materials* in the decorative unit. The line materials must also be of dried plant materials. Treating or glycerinizing of dried materials is only permissible if the schedule states that this is allowed. No fresh plant material is permitted in any form. Accessories are allowed unless prohibited by the schedule.

Two Awards of Distinction may be presented in a Standard Flower Show if all requirements have been met. The make-up of the sections/classes would be the same as listed above for the Tricolor Award. The same make-up of classes as listed above is permissible if only one Award of Distinction is given. The Award of Distinction is represented by a rosette of brown ribbons with gold lettering.

• The *Creativity Award* may also be presented and offered to a blue ribbon winning table setting scoring 95 points or more. The schedule must allow the exhibitor freedom to choose components in those classes of table settings eligible for the Creativity Award. The schedule may not specify what kind of plant materials must be used in the decorative unit, so the exhibitor may choose to use all fresh, all dried or a combination of the two. In designs eligible for the Creativity Award, line materials may be "found" materials rather than plant material if the exhibitor chooses — those items such as plastics, pieces of metal, rope, wires, or whatever the exhibitor wants to use.

For Exhibition Tables, the schedule may not specify how many place settings the exhibitor must use, what pieces will make up a place settings, or what kind of appointments must be used. In these classes, the exhibitor has the freedom to choose and is guided by the class title and the type of meal specified in choosing what would be appropriate to use. The schedule may or may not specify the number of place settings required for Functional Tables. The schedule may, however, specify the kind of staging to be used in any class, and in a plant society show, the exhibitor may be required to use the type of plant material being featured in that show.

Two Creativity Awards may be offered and presented in a Standard Flower Show, with the make up of sections/classes being the same as those listed above under the Tricolor Award. All requirements for Top Award must be met in order for the Creativity Award to be given. The Creativity Award is represented by a rosette of purple ribbons.

• A new Top Award is now available for table settings. It is called *The Table Artistry Award*. It is a *section* award for table settings. In other words, the three required classes making up this section, with at least four entries in each class, must consist of *only table settings*. The section of classes, however, may be of any combination of Functional and/or Exhibition tables which the schedule writers prefer. The award will be presented to a blue ribbon winner scoring 95 points or above. Plant materials permitted will be of the designer's choice — all fresh, all dried, or a combination of the two, as the exhibitor wishes. Treating and glycerinizing of dried materials will only be permitted if the schedule allows. Accessories are permitted unless prohibited by the schedule. The Table Artistry Award shall be represented by a rosette of burgundy ribbons with gold lettering.

This table, seen in Fig. 89, could be exhibited in a section for Artistic Crafts in Division III, Special Exhibits. There is nothing in the HANDBOOK which would prohibit having a class, or classes, for table settings in a holiday show which used Artistic Crafts as an important part of their makeup: for example, Christmas trees or topiaries instead of arrangements — these would be made of plant materials, of course, since artificial materials are never allowed in a flower show; wreaths might be laid flat and centered with candles — the wreaths could be fresh or dried or a combination of materials, depending on how the schedule was written; groupings of packages decorated with plant materials as "centerpieces" — again, fresh/dried/ or a combination of the two kinds of plant materials, depending on the schedule; or there could be kissing balls, either one large one or a number of balls of graduated sizes, suspended above the table from chandeliers, other light fixtures, or some other means of suspension. All of these would be excellent means of providing creative inspiration to the viewing public, and we know that being educational is one of the primary functions of a flower show.

Fig. 89. This is a lovely holiday setting, but it would not be suitable for exhibition as a table setting in the Design Division of a flower show because the two topiary trees used as identical units are *crafts* rather than being a floral *arrangement*. It is a beautiful table, however, and would provide a creative idea for viewers at a holiday show to adapt for use in their own homes. This is one reason people come to flower shows — particularly to holiday shows — to get ideas they can use.
The two topiaries of sweet gum balls glued together and then painted gold are given height and grace by being placed in two gold urns. They are decorated with spiraling red velvet ribbons which provide a rhythmic element. Red velvet birds provide additional color and texture. Placement of the two topiaries, with the two plates between them, creates a symmetrically

balanced design. The lines on the rim of the red and gold lacquered service plate are a pleasing repetition of the lines on the urns. The brilliant red plate and goblet are excellent choices for use with the other components. The metallic gold tablecloth is of compatible color and texture with the gold urns, the brass napkin ring and the gold service plate. The red candle adds needed height and provides additional bright color to this very attractive table. (Deen Day Smith).

CHAPTER 7.
THE BASIS OF IT ALL
THE ELEMENTS AND PRINCIPLES OF DESIGN

The Elements of Design

All arts and crafts have at least one thing in common: they all are governed by the same elements and principles of design. *Elements of design* are the basic, visual qualities of a design, and are the working ingredients the arranger uses: light, space, line, form, size, color, texture and pattern. All of these are tangible, *actual tools* which a designer uses in creating a design.

LIGHT

Light must be present for any vision to be possible. It may be present in varying amounts and intensities, and may be of different types as well, but it *must* be present if we are to see and distinguish objects, textures and colors. Light is basically of two types, it is either natural (from sunlight) or artificial (manufactured). The kind, amount and intensity of light will affect how the eye sees color since light is the source of all color. Diffusion will give all colors and forms a softer, more delicate quality, while highly intense colors will seem brighter and more vivid under more highly lighted conditions.

It is a scientific fact that sunlight contains all of the visible light rays, and when blended together, these rays produce white light. White light can be separated into all of the individual hues of which that white light is composed by separating the rays through a glass prism. Light rays are transmitted by differing wave lengths. Each wave length has its own angle of refraction, so all light rays of the same wave length are reflected as the same hue. Longest wave lengths are reflected as red hues and the shortest wave lengths as violet. The band of color which starts with red on one end, proceeds to orange, yellow, green, then blue, and ends with violet on the other end is called the solar spectrum. These are the colors seen in a rainbow.

There is a wide variety in types of artificial lighting, and the flower arranger may utilize these for special color effects in designs. It is the wise flower show competitor who understands how light affects color, and takes this into account when planning an entry for a show. Knowing what kind of light is available in the show room as well as the intensity and location (or direction) of it are important considerations when planning what plant materials will be chosen for use in designs. Artificial lighting can alter colors since it picks up and accentuates its own hue. Fluorescent lights have a blue-green undertone and a shortage of red rays, so they can intensify blue or green materials, but cause a graying effect to red, yellow and orange ones, making them seem less vivid. Incandescent lights have a yellow undertone, which make blue and lavender flowers seem to disappear in a design. Yellows, reds, oranges and yellow-greens will seem even brighter under incandescent lights.

Candlelight may be used on table settings in home situations. Candles are never seen burning in a flower show for reasons of safety. Since the light from candles is soft, those cool, receding colors such as blues and violets may not show up well, or may actually seem to disappear. White, yellow and cream are luminous colors, reflecting a good deal of light, so they would be particularly good choices for table settings lit by candlelight. In general, pastel colors will be preferable to darker ones in this lighting situation or in any low-light setting.

Lighting can create many special effects within a design, and should be carefully planned and controlled. Since light plays such an important part in our perception of form, color and texture, it must never be an after-thought in our designs, but must be a planned, controlled part of every design. The type of light and its placement (whether to one side or both sides, from above or below, from behind or in front of the design) can do many things: create interesting shadows, which become a definite part of the design, or eliminate all shadows; create an impression of depth; change the appearance of forms; intensify and modify textures; change, intensify or "wash out" colors depending on kind, location and intensity of light. The "mood" of light can be bright, sparkling and gay, or it can be dark, depressing, and forbidding.

Any texture, whether smooth or rough, dull or shiny will be seen in relation to how the surface planes reflect or block light. Shadows created by the type and source of light will intensify apparent surface roughness. If shadows are eliminated by diffusion of light, then apparent smoothness is the result. No surface can *absorb* all light rays and nothing can *reflect* all light rays. Any object, because of its surface quality, which absorbs nearly all light will appear to be black. Black is called a *saturated* color because it has absorbed the greatest possible amount of light. Conversely, white is called *luminous* because it reflects as many light rays as possible.

Designs may be given a reflective quality by including certain hard, smooth surfaces, such as mirrors, polished metals, glass, certain plastics , or even water within the design. The effect can be an exciting one, that of light seeming to shine through the design. Transparent or semi-transparent materials can also be used in a design as transmitters of light, creating still another dramatic effect within a design through the planned and controlled use of light.

Use of any special lighting in flower shows will be determined by the schedule, particularly if there is a need for the supplying of electricity.

SPACE

Space is also an important part of designs and should not be left to chance. We are surrounded by space, and flower arrangements are all the better when planned incorporation of space is a part of them. Space, the open areas in and around a design, is created by lines and forms, and it can be manipulated and utilized to make designs more rhythmic, have more dynamic and dramatic impact, and enhance apparent depth. The sculptor, Auguste Rodin, described sculpture as being "the art of the hole and the lump". In its most literal terms, this could also be said of flower arrangements.

When we create a design we do not have unlimited or undefined space. Space as it impacts a design is either real or suggested, but it will have actual or visual limits and boundaries placed upon it. When we talk about using space in designing, we must first consider the *total space* we will have to work with in a flower show. This will be determined by the schedule writers and the Staging Committee, since they will decide how much space is to be allotted to each exhibitor in every class. Flower arrangers work within a three-dimensional volume of space, their total available space, which has dimensions of height, width and depth.

In a class or section of Functional Table Settings, the dimensions of the table will determine the amount of space each exhibitor will have for staging an exhibit. For Exhibition Settings, the schedule will state the dimensions of each exhibitor's space. An exhibitor in a show has absolutely no control over the total space, but still will need to consider it when planning a design, so that proportions will be correct for conformance as well as being aesthetically pleasing. In the home, total space will be determined by where a design is to be placed, i.e., if it is on a certain table or portion of a table, next to a lamp and under a painting, then total space for a design is determined by the presence and dimensions of those limiting components. This total space can be changed somewhat by moving or removing such things as furniture, accessories, etc. For a table setting in the home, the entire room setting for the table must be considered as part of the total space.

We also consider *spaces within the components* we have chosen to use in the design, such as container, base, accessory or feature, plant materials and staging devices. These spaces can be manipulated and changed by pruning or reshaping of plant materials (by manipulating into certain shapes, such as loops or triangles, for instance), or by elevating a design to create more space beneath it, or by constructing staging devices which have planned enclosed spaces within them.

We as arrangers have control over this type of space through choice and selection of components. We can always choose those which have more or less space within them in order to achieve the desired effect. Instead of a solid, compact marigold, zinnia or dahlia, we might choose to use a Dutch iris or Bird of Paradise. Instead of a solid, straight cylinder or pillar, we might choose a modern container with numerous holes or openings, or for a more traditional design, we might choose one with prominent handles or one which is footed. We might use frames, or frames within frames, instead of a solid columnar pedestal to stage a design. The same would be true of accessories or features — they, too, may have enclosed spaces within them. Bases might have legs, scrolled-ends or feet rather than being flat. Consciously made decisions will provide for the inclusion of interesting spaces within the final result of our designing efforts.

The final type of space with which an arranger must deal is *spaces created within the design*. This is the one type of space over which the arranger has complete control, since the development of spaces and solids are created by placement of lines and forms within the design. These placements determine sizes, shapes and limits of spaces.

The use of space can greatly affect the rhythm within a design. Spaces play a controlling part in directing involuntary eye movement, so spaces can influence the kind of movement as well as tempo of movement within a design. This tells us that space also greatly affects balance, since spaces are important, as are the solids, in controlling the visual stability of a design. In the final analysis, though, spaces cannot balance solids. Introduction of space can also be a tool for adjusting proportions of the overall design. The sizes and locations of spaces will control proximity of colors and textures to each other, determining how the eye perceives them.

We always start within the limitations of the total space, and then create individual spaces within it by the manner in which we choose, and then organize the chosen components. Each element and principle will in turn act and react upon the others.

Space can be a tool for interpretation of feelings and emotions. The amounts, kinds and locations of space can have symbolic meaning: designs incorporating a good deal of space within them can have a feeling of sparseness or stinginess, of tranquillity, restraint and reflection, while those designs consisting of large quantities of plant materials and incorporating few spaces can convey abundance, exuberance, or heaviness and busyness.

Color and texture of spaces are determined by the background against which they are seen and by other objects adjacent to the space. In the case of a table setting, the tablecloth is usually the background against which components are seen, with the possible exception of the decorative unit. The decorative unit would not be looked down upon unless it was a very low, horizontal type of design, so its background would not necessarily be the tablecloth. Its background would be the walls or other features of the room itself, such as doors and windows.

Think of a space as having all of the same characteristics of a form. It is present to some extent in most plant materials and other components used in a design. It is measurable, thus space can be said to have size; space has color and texture, as do forms, depending on what color and texture is seen through and behind the space; and space has shape — it can be determined upon observation and analysis whether it's shape is geometric or irregular.

Shapes of spaces need to be varied enough in a design that they add interest, but the creation of so many different shapes of spaces, causing a lack of dominance and creating visual confusion in the design, must be avoided. Introducing space without purpose, and to the detriment of the overall design is not a positive contribution and must be penalized.

We tend to think of the use of space within floral designs as being important in, and confined to, creative designs. It is very true, however, that incorporation of space is also important in traditional designs. Incorporating space and isolating individual flowers within it enable us to see and appreciate the varied forms of all of the different plant materials used in traditional designs. It might be said that the proportion of solids to spaces can determine the nature and character of a design. Space can give designs an airier, more open look, freeing them from the dense, packed look of the past which often lacked movement and grace.

Designers practicing the Oriental style of arranging have always shown an appreciation of space, while this same appreciation was a later arrival in Western floral design. We have come to understand that space can give a sense of order, grace and meaning to our designs, with its attendant elimination of unnecessary "clutter". Knowing the many ways in which the use of space can influence perception of the other elements and principles of design should inspire us to use space carefully and thoughtfully.

LINE

Line is the visual path through the design. Line is considered to be the foundation of design since lines are used to create the skeleton or structural outline of a design. Technically speaking, a pure line is the extension of a point and has only one dimension, which is length. Lines provide directional movement by forcing the eye to move along its length, thus establishing rhythm within a design. This directional movement can be actual, implied, continuous or "broken" (i.e., visually interrupted in some way). Because lines "move", they are very expressive elements of design.

The character and types of lines can be used to establish a mood or to interpret a feeling or emotion. Down-curving lines may be restful in feeling, or they may also be depressing, sorrowful and weary; up-turning lines are usually gay and lively; gently curving lines are graceful and feminine, or they may seem lazy, slow and aimless; vertical lines can convey a sense of dignity, of inspiration, poise, balance, integrity and of strength; horizontal lines are usually restful, serene, calm, and quiet; oblique lines and spiraling ones are forceful and exciting; diagonal lines are active, powerful, can suggest unbalance and a feeling of falling over, or can show resistance or insecurity, while zigzagging lines are usually disturbing, dynamic, restless, agitated or indecisive — as you can see, line truly has a language of its own. Contemporary creative thought has freed the designer to use crossing lines and lines emerging from more than one point within the design if this is done for a reason, rather than just being the result of haphazard placement. The employment of these lines can often increase a sense of depth.

Lines are characterized as being long or short, thick or thin, straight or curved, delicate or bold. A line which creates a cone, circle, or oval is said to be a line of geometric curve, since it is a line which brings the eye back to its starting point. This is a line which always encloses space. A crescent or zigzag are lines which only partially enclose space.

The most important line in any arrangement is the one which has the strongest visual attraction. This attraction may be attained by being the longest, heaviest, most interesting one or the one with the most variation in form or direction from all other lines in the design. The primary line is usually the tallest or longest line in a design, and is the one which is placed first in order to establish the height of the overall design, or strongly influence the width of a horizontal design. Placement of other lines will follow, and their placement as well as their force in the design will be influenced by the primary line. When placing any line, the designer must consider the placement of each previous one as well as each succeeding one, and all must be contributors to a harmonious whole in terms of rhythm, balance, dominance, contrast, proportion and scale.

Any line direction within a design may consist of only the chosen linear material or it can be created through the repetition of shapes, forms, textures, and colors which have been placed in a specific linear direction. Variations within lines can add great interest and distinction to a design. When you think of it, there are no two curves or shapes in materials created by nature which are absolutely and exactly alike. This is especially true of such unique natural sculptures as decorative wood. Each has its own distinct linear form which sets it apart from all others, and gives it a linear structure which can never be copied.

Lines can also create tempos of eye movement within a design. Visually, they can seem to move quickly or slowly due to the creation of visual stopping and starting points, so that the eye is directed (or "pulled") along that particular linear path. Downward lines seem to have a more dominant attraction to the eye than do upward ones, so usually the lines going upward are longer in order to balance this visual pull of downward directed lines.

Placement of lines and forms control the degree of visual depth found within a design. These structural elements control eye movement in both vertical and horizontal directions, stopping and starting according to placement and physical characteristics of the various lines, so they can also be used to direct the eye in and out and back and forth through the design. In this way, both visual and actual depth perception is controlled.

FORM

Form is sometimes confused with shape, but the two terms are not interchangeable, since form refers to three-dimensional objects, while shape (or outline) is two-dimensional. To put it simply, form might be referred to as shape with thickness or with depth added. In the broadest terms, all forms fall into two basic categories: they are either open or closed. An open form has an airy effect, having spreading parts with spaces between its parts. Open forms are lighter in visual weight than closed ones of the same color, size and form. Queen Anne's lace, alliums, lilies, iris are some examples of open forms. Closed forms are solid and compact, with few spaces between the individual parts. Marigolds, carnations, hydrangeas and football chrysanthemums are examples of closed forms.

Other than being open or closed, all plant materials can be said to fall within three basic types. They are either *spike* (elongated); *round*; or *profile* (indefinite/

irregular) in form. For example, larkspur, delphinium, stock, gladiolus, cattails, buddleias, snapdragon, delphinium, Bells of Ireland, liatris, tritoma, sansevieria, mullein, iris leaves, and plumed celosia are all spike, or elongated, forms. These are materials which lead the eye through and out of the design. Because of their tapering linear forms, they are referred to as releasing forms, which cause the eye to move along their length without being held over-long in any one place.

Round forms are hydrangeas, peonies, yarrow, carnations, full-blown roses, chrysanthemums, dahlias, zinnias, marigolds, camellias, alliums, certain rosette-form succulents, oranges, daisies, etc. Rounded forms hold the eye and provide resting points for it, and in traditional designs they can be used to create areas of interest or focal areas. They give stability to a design if placed near the base or the rim of the container. If too many rounded forms are used full-face, i.e. facing the viewer directly, the arrangement will become very static and uninteresting. Rhythm in such designs will be monotonous, with very little movement. Turning rounded flowers so they are seen at varied angles will solve some of this problem, but not all.

Plant materials with profile, or indefinite, forms are orchids, iris, daffodils, Bird of Paradise, some proteas, lilies, ginger, etc. These are forms having irregular contours, giving greater dramatic impact. They are often used in more creative types of designs.

Smaller, composite forms are used as transitions from spike to rounded forms. They are often used in traditional designs, but are seldom seen in creative ones. Transition, or filler, plant materials are such things as lilacs, spirea, sprays of pompon chrysanthemums, baby's breath, acacia, Queen Anne's lace, statice, fever-few, small-leafed materials such as boxwood, yew, cedar, artemisia, ferns, and many others.

If a design is to be interesting and free of monotony, then it must include variation of forms, but not have so much variety that the design lacks unity and the eye doesn't know where it should look first or longest.

Forms may be irregular or regular, symmetrical or asymmetrical, geometrical or non-geometric, angular or curved, solid or with enclosed spaces inside. They can be made to look entirely different, assuming different forms by changing the angle from which they are viewed.

SIZE

Size is probably the easiest of all of the elements to understand since it is defined as the dimension of a line, shape, form or space. It can be actually measured. In any type of designing, however, the concern is with visual or apparent size, rather than actual size. To be more specific, in any art form, how large something *seems to be* is much more important that how large *actually is* in a measurable sense. The element of size is closely related to the design principles of scale and proportion.

A number of factors will determine visual size. Distance from the viewer is one: objects which are farther away will seem to be smaller than those which are nearer. Relative sizes of other objects seen simultaneously can also affect the perception of the size of objects. For example, a spray of baby's breath seen next to a dinner plate-sized dahlia will seem to be smaller, when viewed comparatively, than it actually is. The placement in the design and the angle from which any thing is viewed is also a factor. If there are two objects of the same form, size and color, the one turned at an angle will seem smaller that the one facing straight to the viewer. A form of a bright, advancing color such as red, yellow, orange, and yellow-green will seem larger than a form of the same size which is of a cool, receding color, such as blue, green or violet. White and very pale colors will also cause an object to appear larger than will objects of darker colors. Objects with shiny textures seem to be larger than those of rough or coarse textures because the shiny object reflects more light, and for that reason seems to be larger.

COLOR

Color is probably the most compelling, most expressive, most attention-demanding of all of the elements. Color can be counted on to give life and personality to a design since it can be exciting, stimulating, forceful, provocative, bold, gentle, dramatic, dull, bright or have endless other qualities. We are emotionally involved with color, since each of us has definite likes, dislikes, preferences and prejudices for color.

Judges always have to be extremely diligent that they do not allow their personal feelings about color to influence their judging decisions. Exhibitors, too, must not allow their designs to fall into a predictable "rut" because they prefer using their favorite colors in all of them. Of course, people who are choosing colors for their own home can indulge their color preferences as much as they like, but in designs created for flower shows, exhibitors and judges need to be accepting of all colors if they are well-chosen and skillfully used.

When we speak of color, we are referring to a specific visual sensation, which is the response of the eye to wave-lengths of light reflected from a surface. All color has its beginning with light, since there is no color without the presence of light. The perception of color and its intensity will vary, depending on the type, source, and amount of light that is present. The color that we perceive as a result of these influences is called *atmospheric color*.

We also know that no one color is ever seen alone, but is affected and influenced by the other colors seen around it. If, however, a color could be seen isolated and alone, that type of color is called *local* color. This type of color especially must be considered when planning table settings, since colors found in all components — dishes, glassware, linens, and accessories or features — will affect and act upon each other. Colors can change, subdue or enhance each other, depending on placement within the design.

Color has three essential qualities or dimensions. The first is *hue*, which is the specific or family name of a color. The words color and hue are used interchangeably when referring to the specific identifying name of a color. You might say that a particular color (or hue) is red, or it is yellow, and so on.

Value is the second quality, and refers to the degree of lightness or darkness of the color, determined by how much white or how much black is present in the color. If white is added to a color, the result is a light value, or *tint*. If black is added to a color, it becomes darker and is referred to as being a *shade* of a color.

Intensity is the third quality or dimension of a color and refers to the strength or purity of any particular color. It is what distinguishes a strong color from a weak one. Some art books may refer to intensity interchangeably with the words saturation or chroma. Intensity is diminished by adding gray to a color, which results in a *tone* of a color. The color then becomes less intense and weaker, more subdued. Intensity is a valuable tool for controlling the character of a design or its expressiveness. Subdued, less intense colors suggest refinement, elegance, restfulness, and gentleness, whereas bright, strong colors convey brilliance, vividness, or even garishness in some instances.

Color has a "language" or symbolism of its own. It can communicate feelings and emotions from one person to another, based on common associations within a culture or society, as well as those based on each individual's personal experiences with color. Specific combinations of colors also have special associations for each of us. To all Americans, the color combination of red, white and blue immediately speaks to us of the flag, love of home and country, patriotism, the Fourth of July, etc. The color combination of red, white and green would have similar associations for a citizen of Mexico.

We have immediate recall of certain holidays when we see a specific color combination or harmony. A color harmony based on shades of green calls to mind St. Patrick's Day, while red and white immediately reminds us of Valentine's Day, and the color harmony of red and green is traditionally associated with Christmas.

When considering the symbolism of color as a means to communicate with viewers in a flower show, the following color associations might be used:

- *Red:* Heat, fire, warmth, danger, a sunset, passion, courage, excitement, anger, aggression, the Devil, rubies, Santa Claus, Christmas, strength.

- *Pink:* Seashells, health, innocence, springtime, little girls, delicacy, femininity.

- *Yellow:* Sunshine and the sun, candlelight, warmth, springtime, liveliness, luminosity, cheerfulness, gaiety, youth, lemons, happiness, cowardice, deceit, topaz.

- *Gold:* Autumn, wealth, sunshine, the moon, the sun, ill-health.

- *Orange:* Autumn, Thanksgiving, Halloween, warmth, vitality, action, strength, flames, sunset, bravery, energy, vigor, modernity, excitement, earthiness, cordiality.

- *Blue:* The sea, sky, water, deep space, transparency, clarity, ice, cold, restfulness, peace, tranquillity, piety, inspiration, twilight, calm, sapphires, forget-me-nots, little boys, cleanliness, fidelity, depression, loneliness.

- *Violet (or Purple):* Royalty, richness, shadows, twilight and dusk, splendor, dignity, wisdom, luxury, violets, fantasy, amethysts, solemnity, melancholy, primness, resignation, penitence, Victorian, mystery, refinement, gentleness, reflective, sadness, sentiment.

- *Green:* The woods, trees, coolness, youth, immaturity, restfulness, springtime, envy, immortality, grass, jade, emeralds, nature, relaxation, freshness, rejuvenation, hope, neutrality, passivity, contemplation.

- *Black:* Night, darkness, mourning, depression, grief, evil, solemnity, magic, Halloween, witches, black cats, sophistication, severity, thunderstorms, formality, death, gloom, harshness.

- *White:* Innocence, purity, coldness, serenity, honesty, truth, chastity, delicacy, cleanliness, weddings, brides, lightness, surrender, crispness, diamonds, light, snow, ice. In some cultures, white symbolizes mourning.

- *Gray:* Fog, twilight, shadows, old age, melancholy, dignity, dullness, tiredness, cloudy days, passivity, frugality, subtlety, resignation, restraint.

The thoughtful designer will choose colors to produce the desired mood or emotion. Those colors referred to as warm colors (red, yellow, orange, yellow-green, red-violet) are bold and stimulating, and can give the viewer a perception of gaiety, warmth, action. Those colors which are referred to as cool colors (blue, green, violet, blue-green, blue-violet) produce a feeling of restfulness, tranquillity and peacefulness.

Color also can give a sense of movement, with the warm colors seeming to advance or come forward in a design, while the cool ones seem to retreat or recede in the design. Warm colored objects can be placed in an area (or areas) of a table setting where the designer wishes the eye to stop or be held. If a form needs to appear larger in order to aid balance, proportion and scale, then choosing a warm colored form will fulfill that need. Using the cool colors will produce the opposite effect.

Scientists and color experts agree that there are three basic or *primary* colors, red, yellow and blue, and from these all other colors can be created by mixing combinations of the pure primary colors in varying amounts. This is called the Pigment System. Equal amounts of yellow and blue mixed together will produce green. Equal amounts of red and blue mixed together produce violet, while equal amounts of red and yellow mixed will produce orange. These three colors — green, orange and violet — are called the *secondary* colors. *Intermediate* colors are those found between the primary and secondary colors, and will bear the names of both of their adjacent colors, such as blue-green; yellow-orange; red-violet; yellow-green; red-orange, and blue-violet.

Complementary colors are those which are directly opposite each other on the Color Wheel: yellow and violet; orange and blue; red and green, etc. (The Color Wheel will be found in the Appendix.) There are also complements of the intermediate hues, such as red-violet and yellow-green; blue-violet and yellow-orange; blue-green and red-orange. The complementary colors are referred to as contrasting color harmonies.

Black, white and gray are *neutral,* or *achromatic,* colors. All other hues are called chromatic colors. White in scientific terms is the presence of all color; black is the absence of all color; and gray results from an equal mixture of the two. The amount of these which are present in any other hue will give that hue its tonal value, which will determine its sense of lightness or heaviness, or its visual weight. White appears lightest and black the heaviest. Many people mistakenly refer to brown and navy blue as neutral colors, which they are not. Brown is a dark shade of orange, while navy is a dark shade of blue.

The name, color scheme or color harmony, is given to certain recognized groupings of colors. These are basic groupings of colors which have evolved because people could easily see the relationships between them, and so, have given that particular grouping a name to designate it and differentiate it from other color groupings.

If a color scheme consists of those colors called *split complements*, then the harmony is one which uses three colors instead of only two. If a hue is selected on the Color Wheel, first find its direct complement (the one directly opposite it). The two colors on either side of that complementary (opposite) color would be the two colors used with the chosen hue to complete the split complementary color scheme. For example, suppose the color chosen first is orange. The complementary color of orange (the one directly opposite orange on the Color Wheel) is blue. The two colors on each side of blue on the Color Wheel are blue-green and blue-violet. Thus, this particular split complementary color harmony would be orange, blue-green and blue-violet. Split complementary color harmonies can be made using every hue on the Color Wheel as a starting point. A split complementary harmony is known as a *contrasting* color harmony.

Monochromatic, translated literally, means "one color". A monochromatic color harmony is one which includes tints, shades and tones of only one hue. For example, if we again choose orange, as we did when illustrating an example of the split complements harmony, this time to serve as the base hue for our monochromatic color harmony, we could use *tints* of orange, which would be pale peach or apricot shades, as well as related *shades* of orange, (the darkest shade of orange is brown; tints and tones of brown could also be used, ranging from beige through rust), and *tones* − grayed hues of any from this large color grouping. Monochromatic is classified as being a *related* color harmony.

Some consider monochromatic color harmonies to be monotonous, but perhaps a better characterization would be that it is elegant, simple, and pleasant. Really, there are so many different possibilities for blending and contrasting, even when confined to the variations of only one color, that possibilities are infinite. Additional contrast can be introduced into the design through variations in textures and sizes. Designers and judges should not demand too rigid adherence to this, or any, other color harmony because they will find that flowers rarely have only one color within their make-up. Most have green leaves and stems (some have gray, purple, yellow, red or brownish leaves and stems), and the color of the leaves and stems may not be within the chosen color harmony. Many flowers will have other colors in their centers, and these colors too may not be within the monochromatic harmony. This is one reason why very few flower show schedules of today specify that exhibitors must use a specific color harmony. They are too difficult to achieve and are much too confining for creative work, particularly if no allowance is made for "incidental" color, such as those other colors found within a flower.

Analagous color harmonies are closely *related* color harmonies. A grouping of colors within an analagous color harmony would include no more than one primary color, plus other colors adjacent to it. There should be no less than three colors in this color harmony and it should include no more than one-third of the Color Wheel, which would mean no more than four colors would be included. To illustrate, let's suppose the chosen color is yellow. Other colors adjacent to yellow can be chosen until you come to another primary color on the Color Wheel, where you would stop. Another primary color would never be included. If you moved to the left of yellow on the Color Wheel until you came to red, you would find that the colors composing that particular analagous color harmony would be yellow, yellow-orange, orange and red-orange. If you chose yellow and moved to the right of it on the Color Wheel until you came to the next primary color, blue, then the colors in that particular analagous harmony would be yellow, yellow-green, green and blue-green. Another possibility would be to start with yellow and to choose adjacent colors from *both* to the right and left of yellow. In that case, the analagous color harmony would include yellow, yellow-orange, yellow-green and green. Adjacent colors should always be used, with no skips between them. There are many possible combinations of colors within analagous color harmonies, since the starting point for composing it can be any color found on the Color Wheel.

Triadic color harmonies are composed of three colors which are equidistant from each other on the Color Wheel. If you drew an equilateral triangle, with the points on three different colors, this would tell you what colors would be included in a particular triadic harmony. Some examples are red, yellow and blue; yellow-orange, yellow-green, and blue-violet; or orange, green and violet. These will be made more interesting by using tints, tones and shades of the three colors rather than the pure hues. Many paintings by the Old Masters employed triadic color harmonies.

Tetradic color harmonies are those which are formed by combining four hues which are equally distant from each other on the Color Wheel. An example would be blue, red-violet, yellow-green and red-orange.

Polychromatic color harmonies are those using any combination of many bright, strong, harmonious colors. This was a scheme often employed by the Dutch-Flemish painters of bold and vivid fruit and flower still-life compositions. To avoid total anarchy, one color should be dominant, however. This is true of all color harmonies, and the total effect will be much more pleasing if there is variation in tint, shade and tone as well, rather than using all pure colors at full intensity.

Colors chosen for a table setting must be given careful consideration, since they are an important factor in the overall unity of a setting, as well as being a strong determinant of the table's degree of formality and suitability for the theme or occasion.

TEXTURE

Texture is defined as the surface quality of an object. It is closely related to our sense of touch as well as to our visual sense. Every material has a texture, and these textures will produce varying sensations when we touch them. This is known as tactile value. Texture may be *actual* — in other words, when you touch an object, it feels the way that your eye told you it would feel — either rough or smooth, coarse or fine, hard or soft, glossy or dull. There are, naturally, variations within each kind. Texture is not confined to the extremes, but may be one of "in-betweens" — an object may be very coarse or moderately coarse, for example. Texture may also be *visual* — because the surface of an object is patterned, your eye may tell you that the object should feel rough, but if you touch it you will find that it is actually smooth. There is the illusion of a particular texture being present, in other words, where that texture does not actually exist. Examples of this can be found in certain patterned foliages, such as sansevieria ("Mother-in-law's tongue"), spotted aucuba, or variegated ivy among many. Carnation petals feel silky, but they look rough because of their jagged form. These materials are all smooth, but our eyes tell us they should feel rough.

Potters, painters and other artists and craftsmen can control the surface structure of their creations, but flower arrangers are more limited. We can perhaps change the textural qualities of containers, bases, accessories and features, as well as of some dried materials by applying a surface-coating of some material, but in the case of dried materials, only if the schedule permits this to be done. We cannot ever change the surface quality of fresh plant materials, however. Our main approach to control of textures in our designs will, therefore, be through *selection* of textures. There is such an infinite variety of textures available in the wealth of plant materials from which we can choose that this should never be a problem for us.

Some materials may have more than one texture within their make-up. For example, a rose or a camellia blossom is soft and velvety, while their leaves are slick and hard to the touch. A thistle's leaf is very velvety in the center, but rough and prickly on the edges. On a table setting, a very fine, closely-woven tablecloth would feel smooth to the touch, while embroidered details on it could be more rough. The eye would perceive these variations in texture just as surely as would the fingers. This is one way variation in texture is incorporated into a design.

Texture has a very sensual aspect, with each texture having a "personality" of its own. We may delight in stroking a fur, velvet or satiny fabric, or those plants which have a velvety texture, but we would never try to stroke a teasel, a pine cone or a cactus. We know that they are not particularly pleasant to the touch, even though we may find them visually attractive and appealing. We recognize actual textures through associations with our sense of touch and by previous experiences. We may possibly find certain textures more visually appealing than others also, based on our personal likes and dislikes.

Texture can affect the perceived size or color of an object. The amount of light reflected from an object is directionally proportionate to its texture: rough textures absorb light, making the color seem darkened and weaker, and the object seem heavier; shiny, smooth textured objects reflect light, making the object seem to be brighter colored and larger, yet lighter in visual weight.

The distribution of textures within a design will affect its rhythm, balance, and dominance, as well as the perception of color and form. Shiny or glossy materials attract the eye, so they must be placed where they do not adversely affect the balance or rhythm within the design. Highly polished and reflective containers tend to hold the eye, for example, and make the design seem bottom-heavy. The eye is held there and cannot continue on smoothly throughout the design. A too shiny base or accessory may have the same effect. A very shiny piece of plant material, such as an anthurium, if placed much higher than other components in the design and leaning away for the visual central axis of a design, will give the viewer an uncomfortable feeling that the whole design is going to fall in that direction in which the anthurium is leaning.

Light and lighting affect the textural quality of any material or form. Rough surfaces are enhanced and intensified by the contrast between light and shadows. Turning plant materials so they have varying planes will create this play on light and shadow, which also enhances the rhythm within a design. Light affects shiny materials in the same way, and varied reflections on different planes of those will have the same effect.

Texture also has the ability to "speak" to the viewer, making it a tool for expression and interpretation within a design. For example, roughness suggests masculinity and strength; smooth, fine textures are suggestive of more delicate, feminine qualities (Gloria Steinem, *please* don't call!); rough prickly surfaces suggest anger, confrontation, viciousness; and smooth, silky, satiny surfaces seem to be elegant, sophisticated, and worldly.

Some variation of texture within a table setting is essential if the setting is to avoid being dull and uninspiring because of too much sameness. The mere presence of texture is not enough, however, since texture needs to be carefully selected, distributed, and controlled by the designer if the end result is to be one of beauty and harmony. Contrasts of shiny against dull, rough to smooth add interest since the special quality of each is emphasized and enhanced by their differences. Textures which are too similar to each other do little to enhance each other and their differences are often not perceived or fully appreciated. Variety in textures can add interest and distinction, but too *much* variety can create a feeling of busyness and unrest. A careful selection of textures is essential to the overall unity of the setting. Texture, more than any other quality, will determine the degree of formality of a table setting. In general, the rougher the chosen textures, the more casual and informal will be the setting, while the smoother the textures, the more formal and elegant will be the character of the setting.

PATTERN

Pattern is the design formed by solids, spaces and colors. It is the result of various combinations or groupings of elements, such as various combinations of lines, shapes, spaces, forms, colors, all of which go to make up the pattern as a whole.

All plant materials have a pattern: it may be from the arrangement of leaves on the stem; from the way smaller stems branch from the main stem; from the way florets are placed on the stem; from the way petals are arranged within the blossom, or it may be from the way lines, shapes or colors are arranged within the overall form or object. When we come to know many different plant materials, we can expect to find certain organized and consistent patterns within specific types of materials. We can know that most ferns, for example, have an expected and constant pattern of a central stem with paired leaves opposing each other along the stem, with fairly even and equal spaces between each pair of leaves. All of these traits will be typical of a particular genus or variety, but there may be variations due to poor growing conditions or genetic changes within a particular specimen which would alter its pattern. Perhaps the designer has consciously altered the pattern by pruning, reshaping, or distorting the original pattern of the material in some way.

Patterns within plant materials may change as the stage of maturity of a particular piece of plant material changes. For example, a gladiolus stalk which has all its florets as tightly closed buds will have an entirely different pattern from one with part of the florets opened. The pattern would be more different still when all of the florets have become fully opened. The successful designer must be familiar with many different kinds of plant materials and know what to expect from them. Does a certain plant's pattern change radically as that plant material ages? Will it continue to change even after it has been cut and placed in the design, or does it stop all changing once the material has been cut? Both choice and placement of plant materials must be considered by the careful designer who wants to control pattern within a design.

Variegated leaves may have regular or irregular color patterns. Aucuba, for example, has spots of random sizes and shapes, scattered haphazardly all over the leaf, while certain hostas may have the same color pattern on every leaf of the plant. Colored margins along the edge of leaves or colored centers also form a color pattern. These are all illustrations of pattern within individual parts which may be included into a design. Flowers may also have color patterns, such as streaking, spotting, different colored edges or centers. There may be blending of colors, either at the base of individual petals, throughout the entire petal, or in the throat of the flower.

All components will have either a regular or irregular pattern. Regular patterns in plant materials are either concentric, converging or a combination of the two. A rose, which has a swirling arrangement of petals is an example of concentric pattern, while a daisy, which has petals all meeting at a defined center is a converging pattern. Plant material which has a strongly defined center with petals swirling out from it in a clockwise or counter-clockwise manner is an example of one whose pattern is a combination of the two, both concentric and converging.

Irregular patterns are found in materials on which shapes, spaces or colors are randomly placed within the overall structure or form. Changing the viewing angle of a material or form can also change our perception of it, from being regularly patterned to becoming one which is irregularly patterned.

Pattern can cause problems in the relationship of various forms and spaces.

A pattern can have forms and spaces within it, and conversely, there may be spaces and patterns within a form, or forms and patterns within a space. All of these must be recognized, and carefully placed within a design to avoid confusion and conflict within a design.

Individual plant materials may be combined to create a design, which will itself have an overall pattern. If the components within a design are arranged in such a way that the design has a basic outline of an oval, a circle, or a triangle, etc., then that is the overall pattern of the design. Many creative designs have an irregular pattern or silhouette which cannot be classified as being of any specific geometric form. This is one major way in which these designs depart from the traditional, geometrically shaped, designs of the past.

Components chosen for a table setting have patterns, too. A tablecloth might be printed all over with overlapping circles, flowers or large leaves, for example. This material, then, is patterned. Glassware may have swirling, incised bands, or an embossed floral design, creating a pattern. China may have a motif of flowers, geometric forms, bands, etc. These also are patterns. Every component chosen for a setting could conceivably be patterned. If carefully chosen, these patterns may be harmonious together and create a pleasing whole, but great care must be exercised when combining several patterns. Otherwise, the setting may be confusing, disturbing, and lacking in unity.

The Principles of Design

The principles of design are the basic art standards used to organize design elements. They are balance, dominance, contrast, rhythm, proportion and scale. They provide guidelines, or a plan, by which those basic and actual ingredients or tools, the elements of design, are arranged into a pleasing and ordered whole. If the principles are utilized well, the result will be beauty, harmony, distinction and expression within the design. All arts and crafts incorporate the same principles in their successful execution, and flower arranging *is* an art.

BALANCE

Balance is the ordered placement of components within a design which produces an impression of stability and of visual comfort. It means that components within the design are arranged in such a way that there is a fairly equal visual attraction on both sides of an imaginary line if it were drawn through the center of the design, both horizontally through the center and vertically through the center. This will be achieved by the designer's placement of components within the design. These placements will either aid or destroy that essential feeling of visual comfort.

For example, if materials are placed near the rim of a container, or on a base with no container being used, then the viewer has the feeling that the object so placed has support from below, and thus has visual stability. However, when we place any object out in space and away from its point of support, then we may begin to experience visual discomfort because the apparent weight of any object becomes greater the further it is placed from its point of support. It then becomes essential that there be some other object placed in such a way that it offers similar or equal visual attraction to that one which is causing the problem. This "tool" for providing the essential visual comfort is called counter-balance. Materials placed low, near or at the imaginary central axis of a design do not need to be counter-balanced, since balance is inherently there already.

Weight placed low in a design always helps to establish that needed feeling of stability. If we place *too much* weight low in a design, then a feeling of bottom-heaviness will be the result, so there has to be a happy compromise in the distribution of weight. The container, base, and accessories, if used, must be carefully chosen and incorporated if this impression of bottom-heaviness is to be avoided. A container of thick and heavy pottery would be poorly balanced by light and airy plant materials placed within it. Plant materials must be compatible in visual weight to their container as well as to other components. Sometimes a feeling of imbalance due to a too heavy container or base can be corrected by using taller than usual plant materials with them. Designers must also be aware that space can never balance solids in a design, so these too must be carefully distributed.

Lighting can also affect balance. Light coming from above a design casts shadows below the design, which gives a feeling of weightiness in that area, adding stability and perhaps bottom-heaviness. If light comes from only one side, one side of the design will be dark and the other light, making the darkened side seem heavier. Light from below casts shadows above the design and decreases the visual weight of forms low in the design while increasing the visual weight of those which are higher.

In addition to balance of forms and spaces, there must be color-balance within a design. There are certain general guidelines which are followed for achieving balance within a design. As has been discussed earlier, the visual weight of plant materials will be determined by either size, form, texture, or color, or perhaps a combination of these elements. For that reason, those things (flowers, foliages, decorative wood, wire, plastic, metals, etc.) which are smaller in size, lighter in visual weight, and in color are usually placed towards the top and the outer edges of the design, while those which are larger, heavier in visual weight, darker or brighter in color are placed lower and nearer the center of the design. Those materials which are largest, darkest, or brightest in color are placed nearest to the rim of the container or closest to that imaginary center of the design. The designer must take care that there is not too much massing, or too much dominance by dark or bright colors, so that the appearance of bottom-heaviness or of concentrating too much attention in any one particular area is avoided. Every design must be balanced from top to bottom, from side to side, and from front to back.

In table settings this general guideline for achieving balance will be used in construction of the decorative unit, and it will also be used in placement of the other various components on the table, so that the table as a whole will be well balanced. To achieve this, imaginary lines will be drawn on the table's top, dividing it into quarters. Components will then be placed so that neither side and neither quarter of the table will appear visually heavier than the others. For example, if you were setting a buffet table, and you planned to use a large platter, a big wooden salad bowl, several smaller vegetable bowls, and a copper chafing dish, you would not place most of them on the right half of the table with nothing on the left side except a stack of plates and some glass tumblers. You would be justified in saying that the table was *actually* balanced, if after it had been set, the table did not tilt to the right and dump everything onto the floor. You would not be able to say that the table would be *visually* balanced, however, because no doubt you would look at any table set in the way described and feel that it was much too heavy on the right side. To correct the problem, you might place the chafing dish and the platter on the right side in a descending angle, with the plates in front of them, the vegetable bowls in the center, and the tumblers on the left side along with colorful napkins and a fairly large decorative unit, placed toward the back on that side of the table. This imaginary table would then be balanced in its use of *forms*. You would not be able to say that the last word about balance had been said, however, until you had also considered the placement and distribution of *colors and textures*. The choice of colors and textures of components, and where those things are placed on the table will certainly influence the overall balance.

There are two types of balance which may be used, either in a design or in an entire table setting. The first is *symmetrical* balance, also called formal balance. This type of balance is used in designs and table settings of a more traditional style. In this type of balance, if that imaginary line is drawn through the center of the design or of the table, both sides are as nearly alike as possible due to placement of like or highly similar components directly opposite each other.

An *asymmetrically* balanced design or table setting has different types/kinds of components or materials on either side of the imaginary central axis, but they are things which are more or less equal in visual attraction or visual weight.

Balance can also be defined as being either static or dynamic. Static balance is that which is still, not moving, in perfect equilibrium. This kind of balance would be found more often in symmetrically balanced designs and those which do not contain a great deal of rhythmic movement within them. Identical or very similar objects placed on each side of the imaginary central axis gives static balance. This kind of balance is the easier to achieve of the two types. Dynamic balance is active and moving, involving a great deal of rhythmic movement within the design. The eye does not stay still, but these designs are still in balance if components within them have been correctly placed.

Fig. 90. This setting is an example of symmetrical balance. The decorative unit is placed in the center and towards the back of the table, with two identical place settings placed on each side of it. If an imaginary line were drawn from the tip of the main line in the decorative unit to the table's edge, there would be exactly equal visual attraction on both sides of it, due to the placement of the components as well as to the equal distribution of colors, forms,sizes and textures. The decorative unit as well is an excellent example of symmetrical balance within a design. If that imaginary line is drawn from the tip of the tallest Dutch iris to the center of the container's base, you can see that colors, forms and sizes are distributed very equally on the two sides of the arrangement.

As with all well-executed table settings, this setting is exemplary in other ways besides in its handling of balance. There is a dramatic choice of color, which gives the setting personality and "pizzazz", with unexpected contrast provided by the lime green tablecloth. The color, yellow, provides the dominant note, but with just enough dominance to avoid any feeling of monotony. The use of space is interesting within the decorative unit, and especially within the twisted stem of the container. There are pleasing and harmonious variations of texture and of form. All components are well scaled to each other and to the overall design. Proportions too are pleasing, with the right amount and distribution of components so that the table seems neither too cluttered and full, nor too skimpy. (Deen Day Smith).

Fig. 91. A lovely setting with an air of autumn is a fine example of a table setting having asymmetrical balance. There is no feeling of unequal visual heaviness in any area of the table. The large covered tureen on one side is balanced by the decorative unit on the other side. Glass candlesticks with brass sockets and bases give a lightening touch to the center of the overall design, as does the delicate crystal stemware. The color harmony is especially lovely in this table setting. The Line-Mass design, in which a pitcher from the china service is used as a container, is also an example of an asymmetrical design. (Deen Day Smith).

DOMINANCE

If a design is said to have dominance, then something within that design is stronger, more compelling than everything else within it. Dominance is actually the process of differentiating between what is more important from the less important in the design. To say that something is dominant is not a criticism. There must be a certain level of dominance in every design or it will suffer from dullness, monotony, too much sameness because everything in it is of equal importance to the eye. There will be no zest or vitality in it. If something in a design is dominant, then it captures and holds our interest. In well-conceived designs, there must be some place where the eye can pause and rest before moving on, and this is the result of dominance. We must take care, however, that no one thing is so dominant that it holds the eye over-long and will not let it move on freely throughout the rest of the design, disturbing both rhythm and balance.

The very word, dominance, implies subordination. If something is dominant, it has command over something else, it possesses more importance and more influence than other things. For example, there may be more curved lines than straight ones, there may be more of elongated forms than of round ones, there may be more bright blue components than of yellow ones, all examples of the use of repetition. This will mean that *one* of those aspects of the design will be dominant. Of course, the skilled designer will not overemphasize any part of the design with too much repetition, or else the design will become boring. There must be enough contrast to avoid dullness, but enough repetition to achieve unity.

Anyone should immediately be able to look at a design and determine what is dominant in it. We should not have to analyze deeply, study and ponder, or search diligently, we should *know* immediately what is dominant! If you can't decide, if you first say to yourself, "I believe it is the black base", then, "No, I think it is probably the red flowers", and finally, "Well, it may be the curving line material" – if this is your reaction to a design, then it is a sure sign that the design is suffering from too much contrast among equals, and from inadequate dominance in the design.

Dominance brings that essential order to design. There is necessary cohesion in a design when interest is not too equally divided and when one thing is stressed. Bold and interesting forms, bright colors, and repetition – either of line, line direction, form, pattern, texture or color – are means for achieving dominance, but are not an end within themselves. The designer's skill in choice and placement of components as well as the creation of pleasing proportions within the overall design will be the determining factor.

Usually we are safe in saying that the plant material should be dominant and not the container, base or accessory. However, this reference to containers is dependent on the design-type or style. In abstract designs, it is not a requirement that the container be subordinate. In certain period designs, containers may also have special importance, but they are not usually dominant. If the inspiration for a design is a container or an accessory, it will still be true in all instances, except for the one exception concerning containers which was just discussed, that these components will play a supporting role and not a starring one, and the plant materials used within them will be dominant in its relationship to these other things.

Emphasis within plant materials can be achieved in various ways. We might have large flowers which are dominant because of their size; flowers may be of especially bright or striking colors, or the designer may have chosen an unusual combination of colors; flowers may be of unusual or exotic form, such as certain fresh or dried tropical materials; or they may be dominant because of their quantity in the design or due to their placement in it. Dominance is one important key to outstanding designs.

CONTRAST

Contrast, in the simplest of terms, can be defined as differences, or having unlike qualities. It is through contrast that we can be *aware* of differences if unlike elements are placed side to side or in close proximity to each other. Variety brings interest to all things — to our daily lives, to the food we eat, to the people with whom we interact, and to our designs. Contrast is needed in all things if we are to truly appreciate anything. How can we savor the good times in life if we have never experienced bad ones? How can we appreciate delicious food if we have never eaten any which was less tasty? How can we value joy if we have never been unhappy? Life is like that — so is design.

The whole concept of contrast involves comparison, and of necessity, comparisons between and among unlike things. There may be comparisons of different shapes or forms, comparisons of the visual attraction of different colors, comparisons of dimensions or sizes of objects, comparisons of textures, etc. Contrast is achieved by placing unlike qualities together to emphasize their differences. Of course, the level of contrast may vary. There may be slight variations or there may be strong contradictions. Contrast gives personality, vitality, and that special spark of interest to our designs. All of us become bored by too much sameness, and designs lacking in adequate contrast fail to hold our interest.

Contrast within a design is necessary if the design is to be interesting and free from monotony, but the designer must use contrast with great care and discrimination, or else the result will be chaos within the design. Something must be stronger in the design in order to control busyness and to draw attention to itself. This is why contrast is so strongly related to, and so dependent on, dominance. To have a pleasing and harmonious, yet interesting design, it is impossible to have one without also having the other.

How do we achieve contrast? By using plant materials having different forms, either spikes or round forms or irregular forms; by introducing variety in colors — variations between light and dark values, between warm colors and cool colors, between high intensity colors and those of lesser saturation, and by varying the amounts or proportions of colors used; by choosing forms of different sizes, shapes, textures or colors; by using different kinds of textures in unequal amounts; by using different types of lines, dimensions of lines or varying line directions; and by varied sizes and proportions of solids and spaces.

Contrast will be used and emphasized in different ways, depending on the design's style or type. In more traditional designs, contrasts or differences will be more subtle, gradual, and therefore the overall effect will probably be more gentle, restful, subdued, and harmonious. Most traditional designs may actually be said to use variations rather than strong contrasts. In very creative and abstract designs, though, contrasts may be sharp, extreme, exaggerated and abrupt with little use of transition to soften contrasts. The emphasis here is on dynamic impact and excitement. Contrast can be a strong force in achieving these effects in a design. Contrast, used skillfully, judiciously and with purpose will give our designs needed variety and interest, but should never be a cause for confusion and lack of unity.

Fig. 92. This fresh and crisp table setting is an excellent example of the use of both dominance and contrast. Since only two colors have been used, white and dark green, they stand in sharp contrast to each other. There is contrast in the decorative unit between the spike forms of the foliage and the rounded forms of the flowers. There is contrast between solid-colored components (the dishes and glassware) and patterned ones (the tablecloth). If we are discussing dominance, is there any questions in anyone's mind about what is dominant? The tablecloth! It attracts our eye immediately. It states unequivocally, "I am in control here", yet it is so well related to the other components in color and in pattern that it is a pleasing part of the whole. (Deen Day Smith).

RHYTHM

Rhythm suggests movement, which leads the eye through the design. Rhythm is created by placing components, or accents, so that the eye has stopping and starting or pausing points. Each pause causes the eye to move on to the next pause, and then to the next. For interest in the design, these pauses should not all be too equal and regular, or monotony of rhythm will be the result. All designs must have motion and then rest if rhythm can be said to have been used well.

Basically all designs are categorized as having two types of rhythm: regular, which is repeated and recognizable as having been repeated, or free and variable rhythm, in which the eye is led through the design in an uneven manner. Just as too much regularity and rest is boring, too much movement is tiring and overly stimulating. Rhythm is something which makes its presence known as the design takes shape and must continue to evolve through careful placement of components. Rhythm is not an after-thought which you can come back to and add later after the design is completed. Rhythm is one of those common factors, present in all good designs, which binds the whole together.

Rhythm may be achieved in several ways. *Repetition* of a certain line, line direction, form, texture or color is one way. Repetition of any of these will lead the eye to follow the repeated element. These repetitions will cause the eye to sense ordered movement and will give unity, continuity and harmony to the design. When certain elements in the design are repeated, the eye will only change direction when it has been redirected to do so by some other differing factor. That variation must occur, or else the design will lack interest. There may be rhythms within rhythms (contrasting or conflicting line directions), and these may contribute needed variety and interest, but one of these rhythms must always be dominant. There *must* be a dominant type of movement or the result will be confusion and lack of cohesiveness.

Gradation is another path to rhythm. Gradation is a gradual change by steps or stages from one condition or quality to another. It is a logical and orderly sequence by which extremes are avoided through a series of harmonious, smooth, and gradually accelerating visual movements. One type of gradation is a slow and gradual change in sizes: the eye moving from the largest material at the base of the design through slightly smaller ones, then to the smallest ones at the top. Movement from darker shade or tone to a slightly lighter one to a still lighter tint of a color is another example of gradation, as is the gradual change in textures, spaces or forms. Gradation gives a very slow, gentle rhythm because it is a regular and gradual change. It is a rhythmic tool more often used in traditional designs than in creative or abstract ones.

Radiation is another form of rhythm which is employed in traditional designs. This means that all lines within the design seem to come from one central point near the base of the design in a radiating fashion. There is one implied point of emergence for all materials. Too great a feeling of radiation weakens rhythm since line direction is less definite, thus it is dissipated.

There are various *tempos* of rhythms — they may be graceful, smooth and flowing, jarring and abrupt, or they may be fast or slow . Think of the rhythms we

Fig. 93. This Exhibition Table Setting, Type II, is certainly rhythmic. The eye is led around the outer circle of the hula hoop frame, then continues to follow the circular forms of the plates, and of the circles created by the little wrought-iron cowboys' bowed legs. The looped and curled black painted vines introduce more swirling, circular lines. The placement of the clipped palmetto frond, painted black, and the cluster of shiny red fresh chile peppers attached to the top of the circular frame, reinforces the main line direction. The large red and white checked napkin, however, gives some needed contrast of vertical line, as well as of color. A second cluster of red peppers adds repetition of form and color. (Deen Day Smith).

see in nature as an illustration of this: the rolling in of waves on a beach: these may be gentle, placid, and undulating on a calm, still day, or during a storm, they may come crashing in at varied intervals. Think of the movement in trees — there may be gentle swaying in a breeze, or twisting and thrashing wildly in a strong wind. Picture birds flying: some flap their wings in order to fly, while the eagle floats and soars. Think of the placement of buds, flowers, leaves on a stalk of plant materials. The smallest one is usually at the tip of the stalk, with the medium sized ones near the center, and the largest ones near the base — this is true of both the flowers and the leaves. This gradation in sizes of the parts of the whole creates a certain rhythm. Use of rhythmic tempos is a tool for expression and interpretation of ideas, emotions and feelings in designs. In nature, all rhythms have a more or less recurring sequence, and these rhythms usually move together with many small counter-movements into a larger rhythmic pattern. This is also true of skillfully constructed designs. We have much to learn from the world around us if we will only take the time to observe.

Rhythm should also be present in table settings. The eye should be able to move freely and smoothly without being stopped or held for too long. There should not be unpleasant stopping and starting of the eye when looking at the setting due to poorly placed components, or to poorly distributed colors, forms, sizes and textures.

PROPORTION

Proportion is the comparative relationship of areas and amounts to each other and to the whole. Several of these relationships within a design must be considered. Since all comparisons are relative, compare the quantity of plant material to the container; the amount of space occupied by the arrangement compared to its background; the relative amount of one type of form in comparison to another; comparative amounts of one pattern to another; amounts of one texture or space to another; and the amount of one color when compared to another.

This is not as difficult as it seems. We all make decisions regarding proportion everyday, probably without realizing it. When we try on a dress and we reject it as unsuitable for ourselves because we feel it is too short, making our legs look too large and the rest of our body look awkward and ungraceful, that judgment is based on our feelings about proportion. When we shop for antique furniture for our dining room, and we decide against that tall, huge armoire or china cabinet because we feel it would be too large and overpowering for our small, low-ceilinged dining room, that decision is made based on our sense of proportion.

Artists have long been concerned with proportion in their work. Ancient Egyptians were the first to use proportions which could be worked out mathematically in their art work. This formula was used in tomb wall paintings as well as in the construction of buildings, tombs and the pyramids. They called their formula The Golden Section. Greek mathematicians studied the Egyptian formulas and used it as a basis for their formulation of ideal proportions called The Golden Mean. Builders of medieval cathedrals used similar formulas to decide proportions, and called their formulas "the mystic proportion".

Proportion does not have to be a precise, mathematical calculation, and in most art forms, it is not. Most of us have a reasonably developed sense of what constitutes pleasing proportions, and we can usually trust our eye to tell us whether proportions are correct or not. This ability improves, as does the skilled use of all the other elements and principles, with practice. Many books on flower arrangement will state that a pleasing proportion of plant material to container is material which is one and a half times, or possibly two times, as long or as tall as the greatest dimension of the container — and so it is, but you will find there are many variations and exceptions to this, so it should only be regarded as a guideline, not as an unbreakable, unbendable "rule". Trust your eye to judge what is pleasing and right in a particular design.

The same holds true of relative proportions of arrangement to a staging device in a flower show: if the arrangement is so small that half or more of the background is seen as unoccupied space, then the design is too small in proportion to its background. On the other hand, if parts of the design extend beyond the background, either at the top or to the sides, then that design is too large proportionally to its background or other staging device. In either case, points would be deducted under Design from the points allotted to proportion in the Scale of Points.

The same would be true of a design in a home situation. If a large design is placed on a table so small in comparison that it looks as if the table can barely support it, then that is a problem of proportion. If a design is placed on a table and parts of it extend under and into the shade of the adjoining tablelamp, and the painting behind it is totally hidden, then that arrangement is too large for the amount of space it occupies, and the problem, again, is one of proportion. Simply stated, you needed an arrangement which would occupy a smaller amount of space when compared to the other things with which it was sharing that space.

In a table setting, the amount of unoccupied space on a table, or within the dimensions of any other staging device, such as background, frame, etc., is compared to space occupied by appointments; to the amount of space occupied by the decorative unit compared to the total space of the table, frame, background, etc; to the comparative amounts of various colors and textures, etc. All of these things will govern how pleasingly proportioned any table setting will be.

We are not striving to use equal amounts in order to achieve pleasing proportions, since such a distribution of interest is dull and uninteresting. On the other hand, one of the elements should not be used to such an excess that proportions become distorted and unpleasant in the overall design.

Fig. 94. A dramatic and exciting Exhibition Table Setting, Type I, owes much of its appeal to the pleasing application of proportions. Two colors are used to provide excellent contrast for interest, but yellow definitely has some advantage in comparative attraction over the black, so there is no problem with there being too equal or exact a division in interest. The involvement of space against solids also introduces a skilled employment of proportions. An area in the top corner is filled by a black tablecloth hung from the top of the frame, while the other sections of the frame are open spaces, but this one filled space is of the exactly right amount: any more and the whole exhibit would have been too heavy, any less and it would have been much less appealing. The whole setting is *almost* divided into quarters, due to the placement and size of the smaller frame within a frame, but not *quite,* again showing skilled application of the principle of proportion. The decorative unit contains yellow lillies, tiny yellow asters, hosta leaves and ivy. (Deen Day Smith).

Fig. 95. Cover the two variegated ginger leaves which provide the bold and dynamic horizontal thrust to this decorative unit with your finger, and you will see a design in which the amount of plant material is almost exactly equal to the size and visual attraction of the bright yellow oval container. Remove your finger, and you will see that these two leaves are exactly right in visual attraction to make the proportion of plant material to container a pleasing one. Sometimes the change or addition is slight, but it takes just exactly that to provide what the design needs. The horizontal lines of the decorative unit are contrasted with the strongly vertical lines of the napkin within the goblet. Since the horizontal decorative unit is so vividly colored, however, it holds its own and is dominant over the unit on the opposite side. This is a very contemporary table setting, totally of today. It has great flair. (Deen Day Smith).

SCALE

Scale refers to the *relative* size of one object in relation to another object, such as the comparative size of a flower to the container, of one flower to another, of base to container, of container to accessory, of container to background. In choosing components for a table setting, we would consider the scale of those components listed above as well as others, such as comparative size of plate to place mat, of plate to cup or glass, of napkin to plate and place mat, etc. Size relationships in a table setting should be pleasing without exaggeration or an abrupt difference in comparative sizes.

What do we mean by relative? We can only judge how large or how small something is by comparing it to some other known thing. We would have no idea whether a man was large or small if we had only seen one man in our lives. Having seen great numbers of men, though, every one of us can look at a man and say with accuracy, "That is a big man", or "That man is unusually small". We can do the same in our designing. If we place a large plate on a place mat which is practically hidden by the plate, we immediately know that we have to use either a larger mat or a smaller plate because the two of them are not in pleasing scale, or size relationship, to each other. We are not talking about relative *amounts* (proportion) at all, because we are comparing these things *one on one to each other*, so the problem is caused by their relative and comparative *size* relationship, or scale. Scale is closely related to proportion, but they are not the same. Proportion deals only in comparative amounts and scale deals only in comparative sizes. Scale is measurable, both visually and actually.

Each of the elements and principles of design is equally important in the creation of an outstanding flower arrangement or table setting. All of them must be carefully considered and employed if the final result is to be a successful one.

Fig. 96. In this elegant Exhibition Table Setting, Type I, there is no single component which calls undue attention to itself because it is either too large or too small when compared to every thing else in the overall design. That is the essence of the correct use of scale in a design. If the setting is analyzed according to the other principles of design, there is balance, achieved through careful placement of components and distribution of color; the color, rust, is dominant enough for interest, but not so dominant that it affects the other principles; there is contrast in line, color, and forms; the decorative unit is rhythmic as is the feature used in it, and the placement of components allows the eye to move smoothly through the overall design; proportions are pleasing, with the setting being neither too crowded or too sparse, and all components are in scale with each other. (June Wood).

While writing the text for the book was my responsibility, the illustrations of table settings in this book are the work of two people, Deen Day Smith and myself. We both have our own special styles since we are two individuals with different personalities, but never the less, we do have similar tastes. This is probably reflected in the settings we have created. Both of us greatly enjoy doing table settings for our homes, for competition in flower shows, as well as sharing our knowledge with others by doing programs on table settings. We also derive great pleasure from seeking out unusual and exciting appointments for table settings.

All of you who have read this book are also very unique people, with your own tastes, personal styles and creative abilities. It is our hope that you will have been inspired to develop even more creativity and distinction in the table settings you do in your own home, and in flower shows if you enjoy competitive exhibiting. In so doing, may your lives be enriched.

I traveled to Atlanta to make the table settings which I created for the book, and they were photographed there. Deen also created a number of table settings at the same time, so we had great fun sharing ideas and critiquing each other's work. We sincerely hope you will enjoy seeing them and studying them as much as we did the creation of them.

Hopefully this book will meet the interests and needs of a diverse group of people — those of you who are members of garden clubs, are exhibitors in flower shows, and/or judges. For you, may you have gained some new, needed information as well as creative inspiration. May your every entry be a blue ribbon, or better yet, a Top Award winner!

For those of you who are not members of a garden club, but simply want to learn more about setting attractive, interesting and exciting tables for your homes, we hope this book meets your needs as well. Why not think about joining us in the clubs, states, and Regions which make up the *National Council of State Garden Clubs, Inc.?* You'll learn a lot, and we would be very happy to welcome you.

COLOR WHEEL

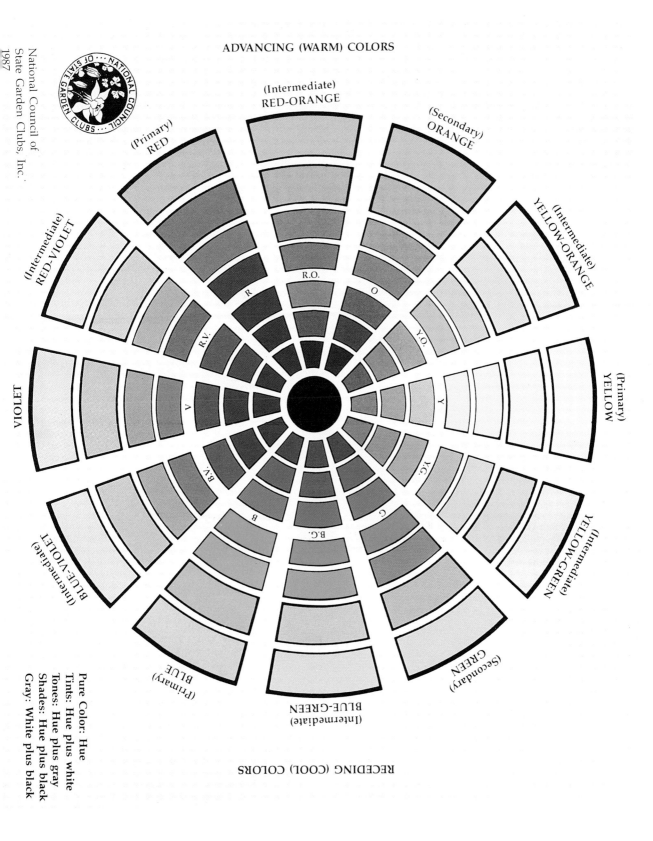

ADVANCING (WARM) COLORS

(Intermediate)
RED-ORANGE

(Secondary)
ORANGE

(Primary)
RED

(Intermediate)
YELLOW-ORANGE

(Intermediate)
RED-VIOLET

(Primary)
YELLOW

VIOLET

(Intermediate)
YELLOW-GREEN

(Intermediate)
BLUE-VIOLET

(Secondary)
GREEN

(Primary)
BLUE

(Intermediate)
BLUE-GREEN

RECEDING (COOL) COLORS

R.O. R O Y.O. R.V. V Y B.V. Y.G. B G B.G.

Pure Color: Hue
Tints: Hue plus white
Tones: Hue plus gray
Shades: Hue plus black
Gray: White plus black

Appendix

COLOR WHEEL

Reproduced from the HANDBOOK FOR FLOWER SHOWS, *1987 edition*, by permission of *National Council of State Garden Clubs, Inc.*

LISTING OF COMPONENTS USED IN TABLE SETTINGS: PATTERN NAMES AND SOURCES

Fig. 1. "Flora Danica", Royal Copenhagen.

Fig. 2. "Stafford Flowers, Spode; Container by Herend of Hungary

Fig. 3. "Bayreuth", Gloria of West Germany.

Fig. 4. "Chinoiserie", Fitz and Floyd.

Fig. 5. "Blue Bird", Spode.

Fig. 6. Frankoma Potteries, unnamed pattern. Hand-made soup bowl, mug and goblet by New Mexico potter, Richard Hanselmann.

Fig. 7. "Duke of Gloucester", Mottahedeh.

Fig. 8. "Swan Service", Mottahedeh.

Fig. 13. Container by Herend, of Hungary.

Fig. 14. Hand-crafted wrought-iron container by Ken Swartz, of Elm Grove, Wisconsin.

Fig. 20. "Maywood", by Lenox China.

Fig. 21. Italian scalloped plate, Pier I. Gold and black striped china salad/dessert plate and mug, "Zebra d'Or", Fitz and Floyd.

Fig. 22. Italian black square pottery plate, Pier I.

Fig. 23. "Fleur de Lys", Spode.

Fig. 24. Wedgwood, "Countryware".

Fig. 25, 26, 27. Portuguese pottery, cabbage-leaf plates. Available in U.S. at Williams-Sonoma, numerous other shops.

Fig. 28. "Canari", Villeroy and Boch.

Fig. 29. Pink lattice-edged plates, Pier I. Rabbit pitcher, Fitz and Floyd.

Fig. 30. China, unnamed pattern. Herend of Hungary.

Fig. 31, 32. Antique RS Prussia porcelain plates, unnamed pattern.

Fig. 33. Duck salad/dessert plate, "Canard Sauvage", Fitz and Floyd.

Fig. 34, 35, 36. Italian pottery plates, all from Pier I.

Fig. 37. Plate, "Autumn Cornucopia", Andrea. Turkey figurines by Andrea.

Fig. 38. Majolica leaf plates by Mottahedeh, unnamed pattern.

Fig. 39. "Tannenbaum", Waechtersbach of West Germany.

Fig. 40. "Tartan", Arita of Japan.

Fig. 41. "Holly Ribbons", Royal Worcester.

Fig. 42. China is an unnamed pattern, made exclusively for Neiman Marcus.

Fig. 43. "Holiday", Lenox China.

Fig. 44. Italian pottery plate from Pier I.

Fig. 45. Corn-motif pottery bought in Portugal. No known U.S. sources.

Fig. 46. "Country Yellow", Johnson Brothers of England. No longer in production.

Fig. 48. Hand-made pottery plate, Richard Hanselmann of New Mexico.

Fig. 49. Thai celadon dishes bought in Thailand. No known U.S. source. May be found at shops selling imported goods.

Fig. 50. Dinner plate, "Medaillon d'Or", Fitz and Floyd. Salad/dessert, "Peony", Fitz and Floyd.

Fig. 51. Same as Fig. 50.

Fig. 52. Shell-shaped pottery plate, Pier I.

Fig. 53. Same as Fig. 52.

Fig. 54. Yellow Italian pottery plate and "Fruits Grande"salad plate, Italian. From Pier I.

Fig. 55. "Anthurium", Porcelains International, Japan.

Fig. 56. Leaf-edged plate, Portugal, Pier I. Lemon pottery plates, bought in Portugal. No known source in U.S.

Fig. 57. "Portmeirion", Botanic Garden China. England.

Fig. 58. "Laure Japy", Limoges, France.

Fig. 59. "Flora Danica", Royal Copenhagen, Denmark.

Fig. 60. "Puiforcat", Limoges, France.

Fig. 61. "Royal Antoinette", Royal Crown Derby, England.

Fig. 62. Italian plates, Pier I.

Fig. 63. "Swan Service", Mottahedeh.

Fig. 64. "Geisha" salad plate, Fitz and Floyd.

Fig. 65. Star plate by Sue Fisher King. Italy.

Fig. 66. "Sunflower" plate, Williams-Sonoma. Black scalloped Italian plate, Pier I.

Fig. 67. All plates, Pier I.

Fig. 68. "Jungle Parrot", Fitz and Floyd. Wrought-iron container, Ken Swartz of Wisconsin.

Fig. 69. "San Marino" Italian plates, Pier I.

Fig. 70. "Taitu", Emilia Bergamin. Italy.

Fig. 71. "Optik", made in Japan for Pier I.

Fig. 72. "Chicken Fricassee", Fitz and Floyd. Black scalloped Italian plate, Pier I.

Fig. 73. Turquoise and purple plates, Italian. No known U.S. source.

Fig. 74. Gibson Pottery, made for Pier I.

Fig. 75. "Holiday", Lenox China.

Fig. 76. Red pottery plate, Pier I.

Fig. 77. "Puiforcat", Limoges. France.

Fig. 78. "Kanesho", Japan.

Fig. 79. A Zato pottery. Italian, made for Pier I.

Fig. 80. Apple pottery plates bought in Portugal. No known source U.S. source.

Fig. 81. Square black Italian pottery plate, Pier I.

Fig. 82. Pottery fish dishes, Portugal.

Fig. 83. Green pottery plate and cabbage-leaf serving dishes, Portugal. Hand-painted vegetable plate, Haidon Group, Japan. Red pottery pepper tureens, Horchow.

Fig. 84. Small blue glass luncheon plate, other glassware, Pier I. Large blue bubbles-pattern plate and pair of birds, Venetian glass, no known U.S. source.

Fig. 85. "Chicken Coup" plate, Fitz and Floyd.

Fig. 86. "Country Gingham" plates, Mikasa. Japan.

Fig. 87. Pottery, Portugal. Pier I.

Fig. 88. "Faisand d'Or", Fitz and Floyd.

Fig. 89. Red Italian pottery plate. Pier I.

Fig. 90. Blue and yellow pottery plates, Portugal. Yellow pepper tureens, Horchow.

Fig. 91. "Duke of Gloucester", Mottehedeh.

Fig. 92. Green and white pottery, Portugal. Horchow.

Fig. 93. Red pottery plate, Pier I.

Fig. 94. Yellow pottery, Portugal.

Fig. 95. Yellow and green pottery plates, Pier I. Pepper tureen, Horchow.

Fig. 96. "Peony", Fitz and Floyd.

References For Future Study

Aaronson, Marian. 1980. 4th edition.
THE ART OF FLOWER ARRANGING.
Whitstable Litho Ltd., Whitstable,
Kent, England.

Agel, Jerome and Shulam, Jason.
Edited by Corey, Melinda. 1987.
THE THANKSGIVING BOOK.
New York: Dell Publishing Co., Inc

Ascher, Amalie Adler. 1974.
THE COMPLETE FLOWER ARRANGER.
New York: Simon and Shuster.

Belcher, Betty. 1993.
CREATIVE FLOWER ARRANGING.
Portland, Oregon: Timber Press.

Berrall, Julia S. 1951.
FLOWERS AND TABLE SETTINGS.
London: Studio Publications.;
New York: Thomas Y. Crowell Co.

Birren, Faber. 1969.
PRINCIPLES OF COLOR.
New York: Van Nostrand Reinhold.

Bridges, Derek. 1985.
FLOWER ARRANGER'S BIBLE.
London: Century Publishing.

—————. 1990.
A FLOWER ARRANGER'S WORLD.
London: Century Publishing.

Coffin, Tristram Potter. 1973.
THE BOOK OF CHRISTMAS FOLKLORE.
New York: The Seabury Press.

Cyphers, Emma Hodkinson. 1954.
HOLIDAY FLOWER ARRANGEMENTS,
   REVISED.
New York: Hearthside Press.

—————. 1963.
NATURE, ART AND FLOWER ARRANGEMENT.
New York: Hearthside Press.

—————. 1963.
FRUIT AND VEGETABLE ARRANGEMENTS.
New York: Hearthside Press.

De Grandis, Luiginia. 1986.
THEORY AND USE OF COLOR.
2nd ed. New York: Harry N. Abrams.

Ellinger, Richard G. 1980.
COLOR STRUCTURE AND DESIGN.
New York: Van Nostrand Reinhold.

Gage, John. 1993.
COLOR AND CULTURE.
Boston, Massachusetts: Bulfinch Press
of Little, Brown and Co.

Graves, Maitland. 1951.
THE ART OF COLOR AND DESIGN.
2nd ed. New York: McGraw-Hill.

Greenberg, Rabbi Irving. 1988.
THE JEWISH WAY, LIVING THE HOLIDAYS.
New York: Summit Books.

Hamél, Esther Veramae. 1982.
THE ENCYCLOPEDIA OF JUDGING
   AND EXHIBITING
5th ed. St. Ignatius, Montana:
Ponderosa Publishers.

Hill, Amelia Leavitt. 1957.
THE COMPLETE BOOK OF TABLE SETTING
   AND FLOWER ARRANGEMENT.
New York: Greystone Press.

Hirsch, Sylvia. 1962.
THE ART OF TABLE SETTING AND
   FLOWER ARRANGEMENT.
New York: Thomas Y. Crowell Co.

—————. 1987.
THE ART OF JUDGING AND EXHIBITING
   FLOWER ARRANGEMENTS.
2nd ed. New York: Privately published.

Hole, Christina. 1961.
EASTER AND ITS CUSTOMS.
New York: M. Barrows and Co.

Ickis, Marguerite. 1962.
THE BOOK OF PATRIOTIC HOLIDAYS.
New York: Dodd, Mead & Company.

_____. 1964.
THE BOOK OF FESTIVAL HOLIDAYS.
New York: Dodd, Mead & Company.

Ingham, Vicki L. 1985.
ELEGANCE IN FLOWERS.
Birmingham, Alabama: Oxmoor House.

Jekyll, Gertrude. 1982.
FLOWER DECORATION IN THE HOUSE.
Reissued by Baron Publishing,
Woodbridge, Suffolk, England.
(Originally published in 1907).

Kroh, Patricia. 1956.
CONTEMPORARY TABLE SETTINGS.
New York: Bonanza Books.

Munsell, A.H. 1979.
A COLOR NOTATION.
13th ed. Baltimore, Maryland: MacBeth,
a division of Kollmorgen Corporation.

National Council of State Garden Clubs, Inc.
1987 ed.
HANDBOOK FOR FLOWER SHOWS.
Rev. ed. St. Louis, Missouri: National Council
of State Garden Clubs, Inc.

O'Neill, Mary. 1961.
HAILSTONES AND HALIBUT BONES.
New York: Doubleday and Co. (This is a
delightful book on color associations and
symbolism. It was written as a book for
children.).

Reister, Dorothy W. 1971.
DESIGN FOR FLOWER ARRANGERS.
2nd ed. Princeton, New Jersey:
D. Van Nostrand Co.

Roberts, Patricia Easterbrook. 1967.
TABLE SETTINGS, ENTERTAINING AND
    ETIQUETTE.
New York: Viking Press.

Sargent, Walter. 1964.
THE ENJOYMENT AND USE OF COLOR.
New York: Dover Publications, Inc.

Smith, George. 1967.
FLOWER ARRANGEMENTS AND
    THEIR SETTING.
London: Studio Vista Ltd.,
New York: Viking Press.

_____. 1982.
FLOWER ARRANGING IN HOUSE AND
    GARDEN.
5th ed. London: Pelham Books.

_____. 1988.
FLOWER DECORATION.
London: Webb & Bower.

Spry, Constance. 1951.
SUMMER AND AUTUMN FLOWERS.
London: Studio Publications, Inc.
New York: Thomas Y. Crowell Co.

_____. 1953.
WINTER AND SPRING FLOWERS.
London: J.M.Dent & Sons, Ltd.

_____. 1955.
PARTY FLOWERS.
London: J.M. Dent & Sons, Ltd.

_____. 1972.
ENCYCLOPEDIA OF FLOWER ARRANGING.
Compiled by the Constance Spry School,
London. New York & London:
Crown Publishers, Inc.

Sutter, Anne Bernat. 1983.
A NEW APPROACH TO DESIGN PRINCIPLES.
3rd ed. Overland, Missouri:
Sutter Publishing Co.

Tanaka, Sen'o. 1973.
THE TEA CEREMONY.
Tokyo: Kodansha International Ltd.
New York: Harper and Row.

The Garden Club of Georgia, Inc. 1990.
AT HOME WITH FLOWERS.
Athens, Georgia:
The Garden Club of Georgia, Inc.

Time-Life, the Editors. 1963.
THE GLORY AND PAGENTRY OF CHRISTMAS.
Maplewood, New Jersey: Time-Life Books, Inc.

Vagg, Daphne. 1983.
FLOWERS FOR THE TABLE.
London: B.T. Batsford, Ltd.

Webb, Iris, editor. 1979.
THE COMPLETE GUIDE TO FLOWER
    AND FOLIAGE ARRANGEMENT.
Garden City, NY: Doubleday & Co.

Index